Reconnecting with Confirmation

Pete Maidment is Youth Adviser for the Diocese of Winchester and youth worker at Highfield Church, Southampton. He has been in full time youth ministry for 13 years and has an MA in Youth Ministry from King's College London.

Susie Mapledoram is the Diocesan Youth Officer for the Diocese of Manchester. She has been involved in church-based youth work and schools work for over 20 years.

Reconnecting with Confirmation

Pete Maidment

Susie Mapledoram

with Stephen Lake

CHURCH HOUSE
PUBLISHING

British Library Cataloguing in Publication data

A catalogue record for this book is available from the British Library

978 0 7151 4208 0

Typeset by Refinecatch Limited, Bungay, Suffolk
Printed and bound in Great Britain by
Antony Rowe, Chippenham, Wiltshire

Contents

For Kathryn
Molly and Joshua

and

For Benjamin, Isabella,
Peter, Noah, Oliver,
Finlay, Grace, Emily and Ella

Acknowledgements

First of all huge thanks must go to Tracey Messenger for all of her support throughout the writing of this book, for her immense patience and infinite wisdom. Thank you to those who have contributed to the book: Revd Stephen Lake, Rt Revd Paul Butler, Rt Revd Mark Davies, Rt Revd Chris Edmondson and Revd Tim Sledge. We're grateful to the Dioceses of Winchester, Blackburn and Manchester for giving us the time and space to be able to get on with writing and research. Thanks too must go to the DYO network for their support in gathering research, particularly to Alice Smith, Angela Heywood, Ian Mcdonald and Peter Ball who are members of the confirmation working group and who have been the sounding board and inspiration for much of what we've written. We must thank Dave Welch at Guildford Diocese for hosting us so generously for two days of writing when the deadline loomed – he served us wonderfully. To everyone who filled in a survey online or answered our questions when we visited your youth group, thanks. Susie is particularly grateful to the good friends she made in the Evangelical Lutheran Church of Finland for their wisdom and hospitality: Risto Korhonen, Merike Perendi, Anne-Katrina Niemi and Pia Korri.

We both want to thank all of the young people over the years who have put up with all our failed attempts at confirmation preparation. We are getting better we promise, bear with us!

Shabba

Foreword

By the Rt Revd Chris Edmondson, Bishop of Bolton

As I look back on my own Confirmation aged twelve, I do so with a great deal of gratitude. I was fortunate to be brought up in a Christian home and to be part of a good peer group, sharing the journey to and beyond confirmation. The genial Irish bishop who confirmed us made the service very personal, and encouraged candidates to come to the service with a sense of expectancy, that we might have a fresh encounter with the living God.

However, this is not everyone's experience of confirmation. In fact, if we're honest about it, the Confirmation Register books of many churches make pretty sad reading. A lot of names appear in their pages who have hardly been seen in church since confirmation day. This reflects one of the main concerns addressed by the authors of this book, namely that confirmation is too often seen as a 'passing out parade' rather than a key stage in the journey of becoming a Christ-follower.

Susie and Pete, and others who have contributed to *Reconnecting with Confirmation*, deserve a big round of applause for the engaging and challenging way they address the issues that surround confirmation. They don't pull their punches, and you may find that while some sections will excite you, others will challenge, and yet others will downright annoy you!

You may not necessarily agree with all the 'solutions' offered, but you can't fail to appreciate the understanding the authors have of young people, and their passion to see them able to express their commitment to Christ authentically and honestly. 'More of the same' simply won't do if we want to address the issue of the numbers of children and young people who have been 'lost' following their confirmation.

Young people are among the deepest and most searching thinkers and questioners, but as Susie and Pete make clear, as a church we don't always take them seriously. One of the many strengths of this book is that the authors have listened carefully to many young people and their experiences of being confirmed. They have also talked with others involved in confirmation preparation and follow-up – whether youth leaders, lay volunteers, clergy or bishops.

In particular they challenge the customary belief that a short course leading to confirmation as an end point – taught by a vicar not particularly gifted in working with young people – is hardly likely to set the average young person up for a life of Christian discipleship in an indifferent and often hostile culture. The authors illustrate this as rather like giving a young person a map, and then leaving them to make sense of the rest of the journey as they go it alone.

The authors ask the reader questions about what it means to be mature in faith, which as we all know is not actually to do with the number of years we have lived. Linked to this they ask those of us in church leadership to take seriously the gifts that young people can exercise in the life and ministry of the Church. This is about a contribution that goes further than the frightening example Susie gives at one point: 'Now you are confirmed you can wash up the coffee cups after the service'!

I love the way, too, in which in the book encourages us to see the positives of adolescence, as well as some of the challenges and difficulties faced by young people growing up in the twenty-first century. The chapter on 'Rites of Passage' is for me one of the highlights of the book. Here is rightly illustrated the way in which rites of passage in other religions, such as Judaism, require far more preparation and seem to mean more to the candidates and the community than is often the case in confirmation in the Church of

England. Thankfully, as you will discover in the book, there is evidence that more churches and schools are addressing these issues, and I personally have come across encouraging examples of how good practice can help this sense of both belonging and believing for young people.

In some ways this book raises as many questions as it answers. Is there an 'ideal' age for a young person to be confirmed? What are the benefits and downsides of the practice of communion before confirmation? How can we get across better the responsibility of the church community towards those preparing for confirmation, and then nurture them post-confirmation? But there are in the pages that follow examples and illustrations of creative ways of addressing the concerns many of us have about young people and confirmation.

Going back to when I was twelve, my experience of being confirmed was foundational to my ongoing journey, in which an inherited faith became a deeply personal one. As a parish priest for most of my ministry, I found few greater privileges than preparing both young people and adults for confirmation. And, Susie and Pete, hand on heart, I can say I always shared the task with others, and ensured that there was follow-up!

That same sense of privilege is now mine as a bishop – one you will find echoed in the contributions of my friends the Bishop of Middleton and the Bishop of Southwell and Nottingham in this book. Whether it's in church, school, prison, hospital, hospice or home; whether the person is ten or eighty-nine – the youngest and oldest I have confirmed so far – witnessing someone connecting or re-connecting with the living Christ is an awesome experience.

So enjoy this book, but don't forget there is a health warning attached to it. Acting on what you read in these pages could seriously change the way in which you approach and understand the confirmation of young people.

Rt Revd Chris Edmondson
Bishop of Bolton

Introduction

Right. Let's get this straight from the word go. Confirmation isn't biblical. It's not unbiblical – we're certainly not saying that. But it's not an activity that is ever mentioned in Scripture.

In his excellent book *The Rites of Christian Initiation: Their Evolution and Interpretation*, the American liturgist Maxwell E. Johnson reminds us that ultimately being a Christian can be seen as enjoying 'table companionship' with the Lord. We, like so many others throughout history, and those that Jesus asked personally some 2,000 years ago, are simply called to sit with the Light of the World and enjoy table companionship with him.

Jesus loved to eat with people, and he invited all to eat with him and seemingly would invite himself to table with anyone. Tax-collectors, prostitutes, sinners, fishermen and even the odd religious leader enjoyed a meal with the Son of God.

The early Church also seems to model itself on the theme of the meal companion. Acts 2 reminds us that 'Every day they continued to meet together in the temple courts. They broke bread in their homes and ate together with glad and sincere hearts.'

Johnson writes: 'Regarding "initiation" into such a diverse and inclusive "table companionship" in the historical ministry of Jesus, it is important to underscore the fact that nowhere do the gospels record anything specific about rites of entrance or preparation for this meal sharing with Jesus . . . Nothing, not even baptism, and certainly nothing like confirmation, was required as preparatory steps.'[1]

While we acknowledge that there is more to being a Christian than simply joining Jesus at the dinner table (presumably many of the people Jesus ate with would have left the meal without believing that this man they had eaten with was the Messiah), it does call into question this whole bizarre initiation rite we call confirmation. What is it? Where did it come from? Why are we so obsessed with it if it clearly isn't something that Jesus himself directly initiated?

Pete's reflection

My interest in the subject came about in an odd way. I've been an Anglican for most of my Christian life (that sounds like a confession doesn't it; 'hello, my name's Pete and I'm an Anglican . . .'), and so confirmation has always been on my radar. I started to go to church when I was around thirteen years old, and became a Christian some time after that. I was quickly confirmed at school (having started confirmation classes a year earlier simply because I was interested in the subject) and never thought much more about it. Working for an Anglican church for five years meant that I was involved in preparing dozens of young people for confirmation.

My unease with the rite grew throughout that time. I could find no real biblical support for the act, and I became more and more convinced that we were confirming young people who were too young to really be able to make the kind of commitment we were asking of them.

It was at this point that I got the chance to write an essay on adolescent development and ecclesiology for my MA degree in Youth Ministry and Theological Education at King's College London.

This was my chance!

So I set about planning a devastating essay that would comprehensively demonstrate that confirmation was unbiblical, probably heretical, utterly pointless and out-moded and ready for nothing more than the ecclesiastical scrap heap (I'm sure one of these must exist somewhere).

I failed – utterly.

You see it took very little reading to realize that it's rather hard to write off an 1800-year-old tradition out of hand.

I quickly discovered that while the act of confirmation is absent from biblical texts, the tradition of laying on of hands is deeply rooted. While the Bible might not contain reference to the eccentricities of the specific confirmation service we are used to, the impartation of the Holy Spirit and anointing of the believer are both rich, biblical customs.

My decision that confirmation was only suitable for the scrap heap indicated a lack of knowledge regarding its history, and an uneducated view of its purpose.

Susie's reflection

I'm sure that my experience of confirmation wasn't and still isn't unusual. I went through the preparation process and service, without any real desire to proclaim a faith that frankly I didn't really own at that time. I just went with the flow and the peer group. Next thing I knew, I was kitted out in cream and kneeling on the cold steps of the cathedral, still not quite sure why I was doing what I was doing. All that it was meant to mean to me and all that my youth leaders had hoped I would experience merely scratched the surface of my life; this opportunity to make a clear and public declaration of faith was sadly insignificant to me.

And yet today I'm convinced that confirmation is something that can be truly significant to young people.

> My work as a youth worker has taken me through the
> maze of confirmation in varying forms and given me the
> chance to accompany young people through the journey
> of the preparation, the service and beyond. I've
> experienced the joy of seeing young people grow, and
> listened to their promises of faith at their confirmation, but
> I'll be honest and say that I've also felt the pang in my
> heart and reluctantly asked myself the question, 'is this for
> life, or just for confirmation?' It's been tough and it's been
> great and I've learnt a lot, but I think that maybe our
> approach to confirmation has become monotonous and
> complacent, and I'm convinced that the time to challenge,
> change and shake things up a bit is long overdue.

This book seeks to answer many of the (quite valid) questions we
wrestled with as we worked through the role of confirmation. In the
first half of the book we aim to give a sense of the history of the rite, to
examine and explore how the Church has moved from those first days
of simply meeting together around the dinner table to the complex
and established structure it is today.

We explore what it is like to grow up as a young person, what
adolescent and faith development look like, and peek into what life is
like for a young person in twenty-first-century western culture.

We explore the importance of rites of passage and particularly the
importance of giving young people good, healthy opportunities to
celebrate a coming of age.

We also unpack some of the thinking around the link between
confirmation and communion, and Stephen Lake in Chapter 2 helps in
working through the union between these two activities.

In the second half of the book we explore some much more practical
themes. We look at confirmation preparation with help from Tim
Sledge, co-author of *Youth Emmaus* and *Get a Life* and one of the

creators of *Critical Mass*. With the help of the Bishop of Southwell and Nottingham and the Bishop of Middleton we look at the confirmation service itself and see how it can be used and adapted to best suit the young people involved. We look at how to follow up confirmation and most importantly we ask the Church to think very carefully about how to treat the confirmed young person as an adult. And finally we take a look at some of the resources available to you as you rethink confirmation and try to signpost you towards other helpful resources.

Our hope is that this book will be read by people from all parts of the ecclesial spectrum. We hope that the youth worker who tries to dissuade their young people from getting confirmed and the priest who believes in confirmation as a full initiatory rite will both read our thoughts and be challenged.

Furthermore, we hope that this book will make a difference; that young people in the future will be confirmed and prepared for confirmation more carefully and with more passion than ever before and that they take on the adult roles of faith with ever more confidence.

Writing a book with multiple voices brings its challenges. As far as possible we have tried to write the book as 'we' and where there are personal reflections we have made that clear with a change of font and an introduction. A few chapters are very clearly written with either Pete or Susie's voice; in these instances we have made this clear at the start of the chapter.

Chapter 1

How Have We Got to Where We Are?

Pete Maidment

This, then, is the setting of the scene. A chance to unwrap the complex history of confirmation, to follow the highs and lows of its (often tortuous) journey through history, and to picture what we mean by confirmation today. No challenge then . . .

A brief history of confirmation

The American priest and liturgist Ruth A. Meyers's book *Continuing the Reformation* contains a brilliant brief history of confirmation, which we have leaned on heavily for this section, with thoughts and reflection from other writers along the way.

Biblically, Christian initiation starts and ends with baptism. John's baptism, as documented at the start of each of the Gospels, was a baptism of repentance and preparation, of putting off an old life in order to be ready for the One who would come after. Jesus' baptism was a baptism of new life, literally a symbol of dying and being born again (John 3).

Christ himself was baptized as he entered his public ministry, not for him as a sign of a need for repentance, but rather as a demonstration of his desire to understand and relate to the human condition fully. In baptism Christ draws alongside us.

Later, in Matthew 28 and Mark 16, Jesus sends out his disciples to proclaim the good news, make disciples and baptize in the name of the Father and of the Son and of the Holy Spirit. And after his death, resurrection and ascension the disciples continue to baptize in his name, teaching that in order to be a Christian you must '. . . repent, and be baptized . . . and you will receive the gift of the Holy Spirit' (Acts 2.38–39).

The early Church, explains Meyers, had a 'single initiatory rite'.[1] The subsequent history of the rite is quite difficult to follow. Practices and habits have changed regularly over the centuries, with the current practice we call confirmation being little more than a couple of hundred years old but with hundreds more years of practice going before it.

The controversy surrounding the rite has several different focuses. Not surprisingly age has always been an issue: should churches confirm the young but risk them not understanding what it is that they are being confirmed into? Or should they wait until the child has become mature enough to be able to make an informed commitment and risk them leaving the church before that time comes?

The meaning of confirmation has also been under constant scrutiny: should it be viewed as a completion of baptism and therefore the second half of a two-stage initiation rite? Or is it simply the chance for an adolescent to make an adult stand for faith and to have the opportunity to own for themselves the faith into which they had been initiated as a child?

Confirmation has also had a tricky relationship with the Eucharist: should it be viewed as an entrance exam to be passed before the young person can be permitted to take the Eucharist? Or is it not necessary to link the two?

It is very difficult to find any evidence that points to confirmation (as we currently understand it) being a necessary part of Christian initiation. In fact wherever it has been viewed this way it has almost certainly been due to a lack of understanding of the full importance of baptism. Baptism is the only requirement for initiation to the Christian faith. It's what Jesus did (Matthew 3.13, Mark 1.9, Luke 3.21), it's what he taught (Matthew 28.19, Mark 16.16), and it's what he instructed his disciples to do (John 4.1–2).

Current initiation practices in the Anglican church are prescribed by *Common Worship: Christian Initiation*. This liturgical document makes it clear that baptism brings full initiation to the Church. As a theological framework, *Common Worship* offers baptism as:

- **separation** from this world – that is, the world alienated from God, and

- **reception** into a universal community centred on God, within which

- his children can **grow** into the fullness of the pattern of Christ, and

- a community whose **mission** is to serve God's Spirit in redeeming the world.[2]

It further asserts that there is '. . . only one baptism which brings people into relationship with Christ and his Church'.[3]

There remains some debate as to when the Holy Spirit is gifted to a person, whether it's in baptism itself or whether it is after baptism in a subsequent laying on of hands or even whether the Holy Spirit comes at a time undictated by either of these two activities. We shall explore this in more detail later in this chapter, but it seems that most of the theology that defends a separate second half of the initiation rite in confirmation has been written in order to defend an existing practice, rather than the practice stemming from the theology.

While there is no documented initiation rite outlined in the New Testament, it is clear from numerous passages that believers were baptized. In baptism they were initiated into the faith and the Church and the Holy Spirit was bestowed upon them. Whether we are talking about the mass baptism that occurred after Peter preached at Pentecost where three thousand became followers of The Way or examples such as Philip baptizing the Ethiopian eunuch in Acts 8, the process seems to be very simple. A person would hear the gospel, repent and be baptized and be filled with the Spirit.

While the Church remained centred on cities such as Rome and Ephesus it was simple for the leaders to continue to carry out the baptism themselves, even as the rite became more formalized and associated with liturgy. As the Church grew larger, however, the logistics simply became too complicated with the early bishops unable to travel to each and every person who came to faith. The practice changed so that initially a new convert would travel to the city at Easter or Pentecost to be baptized at the cathedral by the bishop. Each believer would come to the bishop who would baptize them, lay hands on them and pray for the coming of the Holy Spirit and then anoint them.[4]

With the adoption of the Christian faith as the official religion of the Roman Empire and with the spread of the Church further and further afield, it became harder and harder for new believers to gain an audience with the bishop. The Church responded by granting priests permission to baptize any who became believers locally on the understanding that each one would come to the bishop as soon as possible after baptism to receive the apostolic laying on of hands and anointing.

Constantine's conversion to Christianity in 316 had a profound effect on the Roman Empire. If you wanted to succeed in the Roman Empire it was worth being aligned with the Emperor; indeed many times in the past, if you wanted to live, it was advisable to think in line with the Emperor. So when Constantine converted to Christianity it should have come as no great surprise that the rest of the empire would quickly follow suit. Anyone in power would want favour with the Emperor and a quick way to gain that favour would be to adopt his religion. So if a wealthy businessman or leader adopted the Christian faith, it followed that so too would his household. As such it was not long before the majority of the Roman Empire had adopted Christianity as its main religion. Adoption of the faith meant baptism and so it was not long until every family in the empire that was going to convert to Christianity had done so, leaving baptism the sole domain of infants.

While adults were expected to undergo a lengthy preparation or catechesis before they could be anointed by the bishop, this was obviously not practical for children and so the rite became split in two: baptism – the first half of Christian initiation for infants – and confirmation – the second half or completion of the initiation rite when time or maturity allowed.

In the West various moves by the Church have had significant impact on the views we currently have on confirmation.

First, we need to be aware of just how recent a development the Protestant Church is compared to its Eastern Orthodox and Catholic forebears. The Protestant Church has only existed since the Reformation of the sixteenth century, and the modern Anglican Church as we know it now only became established under the reign of Elizabeth I with the church we know today being finally settled by an Act of Parliament in 1689.

The upshot of this is that the ecclesiology of the Church of England had centuries of influence from other sources before it finally became established, and while a rich and varied history can be a blessing it also brings with it the complication of so many different views, traditions and theologies to sift through. The formation of our initiation rites has also been much slower.

Our current picture of confirmation is even newer, with the latest thought and theology only being developed since the 1850s. Even today the Canons of the Church of England and the wording of the confirmation liturgy remain vague. Canon B 27 requires that no one be confirmed until they can say the Creed, the Lord's Prayer and the Ten Commandments. If this means that the candidate needs to be able to know the three off by heart then very few, in our experience, are confirmed having fulfilled the legal requirements.

Currently, the Canons of the Church of England state that those who receive Holy Communion in the Church of England should either have been confirmed in the Church of England or should be ready and desire to be confirmed. Those who are baptized communicant members in good standing of other churches are also welcome to receive Holy Communion in the Church of England.

In 2006 regulations under paragraph 1(c) of Canon B 15a (to give it its official placing) made an exception to this requirement in the case of children who are admitted to communion prior to confirmation in the context of an agreed diocesan and parochial policy and there is an expectation that these children will come to a time when they present themselves for confirmation.[5] Only about 15 per cent of all Anglican churches have adopted this practice.

We don't even have clear guidance on the question of age. Anyone who has been baptized and understands the promises they are expected to make can be confirmed, according to church law. In some dioceses this is left to the discretion of the priest preparing candidates for confirmation and in other dioceses the bishop has set a minimum age for confirmation.

The communion before confirmation debate

Five hundred years may feel like a long time for a church to be established, but it still isn't long enough to answer many ecclesiological questions.

The debate over whether infants can take communion before confirmation may feel like a new discussion, but it too is a controversy that has been rumbling away since the early days of the Church. The early Western Church admitted infants to the Eucharist from baptism onwards; in fact many believed that salvation depended on participation in the Eucharist (the church in Acts saw the Eucharist as a mealtime activity for all to join in).

From the fourth century the Church saw a dramatic decline in the reception of communion. Much like today, it appeared that people brought infants to baptism at birth but then had little further church affiliation. This decline in communion reception was further exacerbated in the eleventh century with the growth of a doctrine of sacramental realism – a belief that the consecrated bread and wine became the actual body and blood of Christ. A Church fearful of infants desecrating the sacrament by vomiting after having received the Eucharist responded by preventing infants from taking the bread at all. Then later in the thirteenth century the Church went one stage further, withholding the chalice from all laity.

As attendance at communion continued to decline, the Church in the thirteenth century attempted to stem the tide. Conscious that people still wanted communion even if they had lost their appetite for catechism and confirmation, a council at Lambeth under Archbishop John Peckham in 1281 decided to make the Eucharist accessible only to those who had been confirmed, not with the intent of discouraging communion, but rather to encourage parents to bring their children for confirmation.

Those of us keen to promote good theological reflection in all that we do might want to tear our hair out at this point. It appears that the decision to link communion with confirmation was motivated purely for pragmatic reasons, not as a result of theological reflection. And yet the practice of marrying confirmation to communion is still commonplace for many; the vicar of the church where Pete was youth worker would not allow unconfirmed young people to receive communion at the end of a youth group weekend away for fear of diminishing the place of confirmation. Communion is somehow seen as a reward to the young person who has been confirmed; access to this sacrament instituted by Christ is withheld from children so that they have 'something to look forward to'. Our practice may have the effect of elevating the very human activity of confirmation above sacraments ordained by Christ himself.

That is a very brief history of how we have ended up with our current practices of confirmation but what is the theological and biblical thought behind the rite?

Earlier we did quite dismissively announce that confirmation was unbiblical, but there are elements of the rite that clearly have their basis firmly rooted in Scripture: particularly the emphasis on laying on of hands and the gifting of the Holy Spirit.

There can be no doubt that Christians need to be filled with the Holy Spirit in order to continue in faith. Jesus promised the coming of the Spirit (John 15) and soon after he ascended the disciples receive the Spirit (Acts 2). Time and again the New Testament talks about the believers being filled with the Spirit, or the Spirit coming, and the Spirit seems to come at his own time and in his own way. Not surprisingly as soon as we try to put a formula on what it is that ushers in the Spirit we discover an example of how he comes differently.

It isn't possible to say that the Spirit comes only with the laying on of hands. While there are passages where this clearly happens (Acts 8) there are also examples of where the Spirit comes of his own accord (Acts 2). What can be certain is that the believer needs the Spirit and when the Spirit comes he brings power. There is no question that the laying on of hands is a powerful and symbolic act, and that when a believer lays hands on another and prays for the Spirit to come then the Spirit does indeed come; sometimes to heal and sometimes to strengthen or to give gifts both specific and general.

There is, however, no clear New Testament teaching that says that the laying on of hands and the imposition of the Spirit is somehow the second half of a two-stage initiation rite. In *The Message of Acts* John Stott is at great pains to explain that traditions that use the story of Paul baptizing the disciples of Ephesus in Acts 19 as a justification for this secondary initiation rite are simply proof texting.[6] Michael Green asserts that the disciples mentioned in this passage were in no sense Christians[7] and so the baptism and imposition of the Spirit that happens in the passage are part of one and the same initiation rite, and while F. F. Bruce concedes the fact that Luke refers to them as disciples, a term he usually uses to mean Christians, and that the rite practised in this instance is an 'exceptional case',[8] he further notes that Acts 19 is the only example in the New Testament of a re-baptism, which would suggest that what was happening was not actually a rebaptism but a superseding of a Johannine baptism of repentance with a true Christian baptism of rebirth.[9]

So while the laying on of hands doesn't seem to have a role in the initiation rite in any kind of legalistic sense, it is still a powerful and moving symbol and furthermore is an act through which the Holy Spirit works and moves. Writing about the instruction to go on to maturity through, among other things, the laying on of hands in Hebrews 6.1–2 Raymond Brown writes '. . . this simple form of Hebrew prayer symbolism became part of the Christian initiatory rite. It was obviously related to the gift of the Holy Spirit.'[10]

While it is clear that baptism is a once for all sacrament, confirmation is simply another time when a believer receives the Holy Spirit. The symbol of laying on of hands, and the further giving of the Holy Spirit for strengthening of the maturing believer is, we believe, reason enough to continue the practice of confirmation. Furthermore, that confirmation should involve the bishop simply raises the power of the occasion; while we can't argue that apostolic succession adds any greater presence of the Spirit or any deeper level of anointing, we can say that the bishop's presence adds a layer of drama or dramatic flow[11] to the service which wouldn't be there otherwise. Indeed, the service book doesn't award the bishop any specific sacramental role in the service, but rather charges him with 'focusing the mission and unity of the Church . . . the purpose of the bishop's ministry in initiation is to enable the whole process so that the journey of those coming to faith is protected and affirmed.'[12]

The symbolic gesture of laying on of hands, we would argue, carries a wonderful heritage and is a beautiful image in confirmation. G. W. H. Lampe wonders whether the laying on of hands in Acts chapter 8 had a much deeper symbolism. The hatred of the Samaritans by the Jews is a well-documented fact; the story of the Good Samaritan reminds us of the risk of being associated with one of the hated unclean Samaritans. It's no coincidence that it's the same John who had previously offered to call down fire on a Samaritan city (Luke 9.54) who now places his hands on the Samaritans and prays for them. It's a picture reminiscent of Princess Diana in 1987 holding hands with an AIDS sufferer, dispelling the myth that by touching someone with the disease you might catch it yourself. In this Acts passage John does a similarly world-shaking action, by placing his hands on someone who to that point had been viewed as an outcast.

It might be a bit of a stretch to suggest that we view young people in the same way as the Jews viewed the Samaritans or a 1980s society viewed AIDS sufferers (although young people are often marginalized and demonized in our culture), but the same symbolism is undeniable as a bishop places his hands on a former outsider and welcomes him or her to membership of the Church and invites the Spirit for the ongoing strengthening of the maturing faith.

It seems that we have a tendency in the Church to sacralize things. We take very normal activities and we turn them into something sacred, then because that sacralized act becomes habit and then history, we get caught up in the act and can be at risk of losing the meaning. Two stories will explain this a bit better.

The late great Mike Yaconelli wrote a fabulous book called *Messy Spirituality* which is essentially a collection of stories about people for whom Christianity and spirituality is messy. He writes this story about Michael: the boy who unchained his mother from depression.

> Michael's physical and mental disabilities required him to live in a twenty-four-hour care facility. His parents lived some distance away, and periodically Michael's mother suffered from bouts of depression brought on by not being able to care for her son. During one depressive episode she stayed in bed for days, unresponsive to all efforts to engage her, even her husband's. Concerned, Michael's father asked him to come home to see if his presence could bring her out of her deep despair.
>
> Michael could walk but needed assistance with almost everything else, and his speech was impaired, making his words difficult to understand. When he arrived home, Michael walked straight into his mother's bedroom and sat on her bed. He stayed with her for a long time, but said nothing. When his

father came into the bedroom Michael pointed to a large flower vase and repeated over and over again, 'Ca . . . ca . . . ca . . . oke.' It took his father a while to understand that Michael was asking him to fill the vase with Coke.

When the father returned with the vase of Coke, Michael took a small piece of bread he had earlier found in the kitchen, then tenderly took hold of his mother's hand and placed the bread in it. He dipped the bread into the Coke and gently lifted the bread to his mother's mouth as he began stumbling through the words of the Eucharist. His mother's eyes filled with tears as she took the bread. Within a few hours she came out of her depression.[13]

Michael grasped the importance of Eucharist, he grasped what it meant to feed on the body and blood of the Son of God. This simple act of remembering the death of the Saviour has been complicated by 2,000 years of tradition so that often we worry more about who is giving us the sacrament and who has said the liturgy than about the significance of the event. This is not to down play the importance of the Eucharist, far from it, but simply to ask whether what Michael did with his mum was any less Eucharist than even the most serious and traditional of liturgical acts.

Another story. Richard Wurmbrand was twice imprisoned and tortured for a total of thirteen years for preaching the gospel in communist Romania. Despite warnings and torture and threat of further arrest he never stopped preaching and baptizing, even when in prison. The story goes that years after leaving Romania Richard came to speak at a church in England. The church he visited was going through a long discussion about baptism. They were arguing about whether someone who has been sprinkled with water can be considered properly baptized, or whether one can only be considered to have been baptized if a full immersion has taken place. Incensed by the discussion Richard stood up and explained to the church that when he was in prison and people wanted to be baptized, water was so scarce that sometimes they had to resort to baptizing with a sprinkle of urine. He asked the church whether they considered that to be 'proper' baptism or not and then left the meeting.

Again, this is not to undermine the importance and place of baptism, heaven forbid, but again it is possible that we have allowed our rituals and our traditions to undermine the importance of what is going on. Have we become more concerned with the age at which we baptize and the form that baptism takes than with the purpose of baptism? Richard Wurmbrand certainly grasped the importance of the act and was quite legitimate in challenging the church as he did.

On the Way, the 1995 report of the General Synod on Anglican initiation rites, puts this theory of *sacrelization* much more simply. Rather than confirmation being a 'rite in search of a theology' it describes the problem as the 'over-concentration of too much theology on one moment in the process', namely the confusion over the moment when hands are laid and the Spirit comes.

So how do we conclude this chapter? Our hope is that in realizing the mess that confirmation is in, the confusion that has surrounded the rite over the centuries and the ambiguity that still sits heavily on the chest of the whole subject you can be released to think a bit more creatively about how you go about using what remains an important service and an important moment in someone's life. Confirmation really does have no hard and fast rules, and for every hundred years that it has come to represent one thing, there is another century when it has represented something quite different. We hope that as you read this book you will come to love the richness of the history of confirmation, but not feel that you have to be tied into one tradition or another with its execution. We hope that you will recognize that confirmation doesn't have to be linked to the Eucharist, that it doesn't form the second half of Christian initiation and there is no set age at which it is best to do it.

We have already said that we love confirmation and the reason is that it can be such an important moment in the life of a young person, such an incredibly powerful turning point, not just in their faith development but also in their development as a person. We hope that as you study some faith development and adolescent development theories, as you explore the importance of providing good rites of passage for young people you will find freedom in using confirmation as a benefit to young people rather than feeling that you have to impose a rite on them for the sake of the rite.

It's a big ask, we do realize that, but we also feel that it is an important discussion to have.

Chapter 2

Rethinking Communion before Confirmation

Stephen Lake

Stephen Lake is Sub Dean of St Albans. He has extensive experience of parish ministry and has written on confirmation, marriage and in particular, the admission of baptized children to Holy Communion.

Being confirmed

I well remember being confirmed at the age of thirteen. My family had no real church background. I had come to faith, or perhaps more truthfully, come to the Church, through Scouting. Our Scout Leader was also the verger at the parish church and he had a unique ability of drawing everyone in to the worshipping community. One Sunday after church parade, he called me over. They were short of a server for the next service, and I was needed. So I did what Skip wanted me to do, I did my duty. Soon I had caught the bug and it seemed right to be confirmed. But I had not been baptized. My parents had left that for me to decide for myself. At the time, I remember being an embarrassed teenager at the thought of doing what happened to babies but there was a motivating factor. You see, there was a girl . . . and she was in the church youth club. If you wanted to go to the church youth club, you had to be confirmed. So that was it. Looking back I'm not sure how much these various factors played a part in my commitment to follow Christ, but I suspect that God was happy to work with the raw material in terms of my 'Yes' and to let the rest come along in due course. Thirty years later, I have been an ordained priest for all my working life and will be a priest forever. God has a wonderful way of making the most of what we offer him.

This book seeks to show how confirmation is important and can become even more vital in the future. We have learnt how confirmation has a messy foundation and yet an enduring value. It is attractive that something that has so clearly been used and abused by the Church over the centuries still has such appeal. For me, this is where the truth rests. No matter what our history, churchmanship, tradition, or status, God can meet us and transform us. No matter what hurdles or qualifications we place in the way of those who seek him, Christ is able to call us and to change us. We can trust in what God does for us in Christ, including in confirmation, and the responsibility of the Church is simply to tune in to what God is already doing and to respond with his love and welcome.

In my case I believe God was behind my baptism and confirmation as a teenager. But that he was also behind the love that I found in his Church (not from the girl) and the valued place that I was given. It was that love that kept me coming, and eventually led to a serious and mature commitment. As Anglicans, we believe in all this stuff. We believe that God is there in baptism through grace, as well as in any personal commitment we can muster. We believe that the Holy Spirit can empower us through confirmation and that the Church can and should accompany us along the way.

I have three children, two of whom are teenagers. They have both been confirmed. Their formation in the Church was the exact opposite to mine. As a family we have been fully involved throughout their lives. Instead of not being members of the Church and then joining and staying as I did, I fully expect them soon to have a wilderness time as they find their own place in the world, without the daily influence of their embarrassing dad. But I'm OK with that for the moment, for I believe that God can work with this too and that at some point and in their own time, they will, in a sense, *re*-confirm their commitment for themselves. My main reason for believing this is that, more than their confirmation, the thing that they have valued above any aspect of church is belonging. It is the fun they have at youth club and in services and on camp and in discussions that has brought them to this point and which they will remember forever. Now, when they don't go to church because dad is preaching or because it's exam time or because they've been out too late the night before, what they miss after a while is that sense of belonging to something greater than themselves. It's a belonging that welcomes all ages and where, just sometimes, unconditional love is on offer. What they both say they really miss most if they have been AWOL is receiving Holy Communion. Despite dad's best efforts to teach them, and however much they fail to articulate their beliefs, they do miss receiving communion. For them, this sign above all others is the sign of belonging to the Church and belonging to Christ. In receiving communion their faith is confirmed. There are many historical and theological reasons for confirmation and communion becoming entwined, and there may be good reasons for this being the case. God is still able to work with that and make us his own.

Both these patterns of approaching confirmation have their merits and drawbacks. But what we see is that belonging has a crucial role to play in any sense of personal commitment. Confirmation provides an ideal opportunity for this sense of belonging. One is founded in baptism and then quite literally confirmed. So church should see its role around confirmation as enabling this sense of real and tangible belonging. However much we wander in the future, we will still belong and feel more able to reconnect. Crucially, if receiving Holy Communion has been normal to us then we are more likely to return and to recognize what we have been missing. If we are to rethink confirmation as Pete and Susie suggest, then we need to understand its connection with, but not control of, communion too. Confirmation, and more fundamentally baptism and Holy Communion all have their role and place in the life of the Anglican Church and in the lives of Christians. They are all interconnected certainly, but they each exist to the glory of God and the gift of his people and they must not be confused or conflated.

When I was confirmed all those years ago, I received baptism, confirmation and communion all in the one rite, from the bishop who subsequently married and ordained me. Therefore to receive communion was normal for me, not a reward. I had nothing else really. In *Reconnecting with Confirmation* we seek to give thanks for baptism, affirm confirmation and release communion, all to acknowledge what God is doing for us in Christ.

Understandings of confirmation

Common Worship acknowledges the complications around confirmation in the Western Church and notes its different and overlapping senses. But these five points do summarize well what we believe confirmation is and can be for.

- *To establish or secure.* This is the earliest and non-technical sense. It is used of an action in which the Church accepts and acts on baptism. It was applied to the first receiving of communion as well as to episcopal anointing and hand-laying.

- *A post-baptismal episcopal rite.* In the ninth century this technical sense attached itself to the exclusively western practice of a post-baptismal episcopal rite. There has been a continuing debate in the West as to whether this 'confirmation' consists of the general prayer for the sevenfold gift of the Spirit said over all the candidates or the specific act of praying for each candidate that follows the general prayer.

- *To strengthen.* This understanding of the episcopal rite became widespread in the thirteenth century, having been applied earlier to an adult's need for strength to witness and to resist temptation, and then transferred to children as they approach adulthood.

- *To approve or recognize.* In Cranmer's rites the bishop's action is seen as signifying the Church's recognition of the personal faith nurtured in the catechetical process.

- *To ratify.* The meaning of individual or personal ratification emerges in the preface added to the confirmation service in *The Book of Common Prayer* (1662).

In an episcopally ordered Church therefore, where the bishop is the chief minister of the whole process of Christian initiation, his role is integral to its practice and vital to the candidate. The Church of England wishes to maintain this ministry. Therefore we can re-think confirmation in these terms, affirming the link with Holy Baptism and acknowledging the connection with Holy Communion but not its necessity as a qualification. Confirmation is about establishing and securing, strengthening with a post baptismal rite by a bishop, the approving and recognizing of a candidate and the ratification of their place in the life of the Church.

Food for the journey

In 2009 there was a brief scare involving swine flu. We probably all knew of people who had travel plans disrupted and we may even know of some who fell ill. In the end the fear of a widespread epidemic was largely unrealized, either because the plans put in place for such an event were successful, or because the virility of the illness was less than expected.

The Anglican Church erred on the side of caution, however, and published recommendations that congregations should refrain from sharing the chalice while there was still a risk of epidemic and so for the first time in many years churches up and down the country took communion in one kind.

For many, the experience was not negative. They were reminded that communion as a symbol wasn't lessened by this reduction, and that, at least theologically speaking, taking just the body was still receiving the full Eucharist; you cannot receive part of Christ's eucharistic gift, you receive Christ himself.

What was so interesting was the reaction of the people. Congregations understood the theological implication, but they did not like it. Nor should they. Having something so familiar withdrawn had a big impact. It made people think. It made them consider what they believe about the Eucharist and in particular about receiving communion. It jolted many in regular congregations to realize just how important their worship is and how special receiving communion is to them. It made many of us realize what we take for granted. Having something withdrawn from you often promotes a reaction.

Losing an element of Holy Communion makes us reconsider why it is important to us and why Jesus gave us this powerful gift. Most impressively, a number of people have discussed with me that, perhaps for the first time, they have discovered in themselves just how important this sacrament is, and that by definition it should never be withheld, withdrawn or qualified for admission. If baptism is all we need for entry into Christ and to share in the sacraments, then this must include access to communion. Confirmation is the public rite of mature commitment before a bishop, not the moment of admission to Holy Communion. Perhaps once again, God is able to use our human frailties and decisions to show us a deeper understanding.

So to be sure, what do we understand about all sharing in the Eucharist? At the Last Supper Jesus gave his disciples signs to remember him by. Following the events of Good Friday and Easter Day, the disciples realized that Jesus had been sharing, not just bread and wine, but himself – his body and his blood – as a living remembrance of him and his saving work. Every time we celebrate the Eucharist we enter again into the mystery of Christ's sacrifice, as we encounter him in word and sacrament.

The first Christians gathered in each other's homes to celebrate the Eucharist together, often in secret. Christians all over the world still come together to worship in homes, hospitals, churches and cathedrals. We gather as individuals, with all our cares and concerns, our joys and sorrows, and in our offering of praise and thanksgiving, Christ makes us one body.

We confess our sins and receive the assurance of God's forgiveness. We break open the Scriptures together, and hear anew the story of God's saving acts. We affirm the faith that has been passed on down the centuries, and which we are called to proclaim afresh today. And we bring to God the concerns of the world, the church, our community, and ourselves – because in the Eucharist we are called to bring all things to God, whose will is to reconcile all things to himself.

In the Eucharist we mirror the action of Christ himself at the Last Supper. We *take* the bread and wine, gifts from among all God has given us, and symbols of our offering of ourselves to God. We ask God to *bless* the gifts, using the words Jesus gave us, so that he may be present among us. Just as his body was broken, we *break* the bread to acknowledge our own brokenness and dependence on God's forgiveness. And we *share* the bread and wine: Christ's gift of himself to us enables us to share in the life of God, and reminds us that we belong to him and to each other.

At the end of the Eucharist, we are sent out to live as members of the Eucharistic community in the world. The Saviour of the World comes to us in each and every celebration. As we are fed by him, we are called, once again, to be signs of his love in the world: receiving the body of Christ, we are sent out to *be* the body of Christ.

Passing out?

One of the greatest realizations of the Church of England in recent years has been to admit baptized children to Holy Communion. If confirmation is not the gateway to receiving communion, baptism must be, regardless of age. In 2006 the Church of England agreed rules to admit baptized children to communion. In typically Anglican fashion, this movement of the Spirit became legislation. Since then a steadily growing number of parishes have moved towards including children in the Eucharist. There were some fears this move might destabilize confirmation but anecdotal evidence at this stage suggests the opposite. Certainly, in my experience, the sharing of communion at an early age is of benefit to church and communicant alike and the child feels more a part of the worshipping community. Rather than make confirmation unnecessary, it seems at this early stage that children are being retained in the Church and that confirmation is becoming more valued as that maturing rite of recognition and public affirmation. Certainly at St Albans Cathedral, where children were admitted in 2002 (under specific permission) the experience has been that confirmation numbers have grown but young people are choosing to be confirmed older than the previous average age of around eleven. In fact they are choosing to be confirmed around the fourteen- to fifteen-year-old mark and this seems to be an increasing trend. Confirmation is and will be a much more powerful mission opportunity for the church if this is to be replicated elsewhere.

In 2006 I wrote *Let the Children Come to Communion*.[1] It promoted the new legislation and provided a mission tool for parishes. If we are to understand the unnecessary link between confirmation and communion, we must comprehend the equal and opposite importance of sharing communion with all the baptized, especially children. The Archbishop of Canterbury wrote in the Foreword:

> For a steadily growing number of local Anglican communities, the admission of children to Holy Communion is becoming a central part of their mission strategy. It is a practice that affirms the seriousness with which the Church takes its younger members (*not* 'the Church of the future', as the hackneyed phrase goes, but an intrinsic element in the Church of the present). It takes for granted that children need as believers what adults need – nurture, listening, stretching of the mind and heart. It moves decisively away from the deeply rooted assumption that adolescence is the best moment to make the transition into full visible participation in the sacramental life of the Church – a rather questionable presupposition at the best of times; and so it offers some viable alternative to the 'Confirmation as passing out parade model' which is the sad reality in many places.

It is this sense of 'passing out parade' that has been a feature of confirmation for so long. As Archbishop Rowan says, these concepts are 'deeply rooted'. So to understand confirmation as a maturing rite of commitment – literally, confirmation of something in place – requires a corresponding understanding of the importance of the admission of children to Holy Communion, to 'full visible participation in the sacramental life of the church'. As you may be coming to *Reconnecting with Confirmation* with new eyes, the authors have asked me to give here an overview of the admission of baptized children to Holy Communion. The two, in many ways, go hand in hand.

We will look with greater detail at this understanding of confirmation as a passing out parade in Chapter 6.

Scripture and communion for all the baptized

Of course, just as there is no explicit description of confirmation as we understand it in Scripture, there is no explicit command from Christ or the New Testament Church to share communion with children and young people. But this is assumed and indeed generally understood. Jesus himself was very clear indeed about his view of children and their place in the kingdom.

Throughout the Old Testament, children are seen as a gift from God and a sign of the covenantal relationship with him. The future of Israel is secured by the gift of children and God is fully involved in the heritage and development of children. A good example is the gift of Isaac to Abraham. Isaac is the child of promise, of future hope but also through Abraham's testing (Genesis 22), the child of innocence and obedience. In Exodus, when the people are led through the wilderness and fed by the manna from heaven, this is for the whole community, not just the adults. Just as all the people crossed the Red Sea, so God includes all in his goodness. In 1 Samuel 2, the boy was dedicated to the Lord and a model of faithfulness. God called and Samuel responded and in time became the leading prophet in Israel. The boy is the mouthpiece of God and a symbol of innocent obedience, a model of call and response. The child brings that rare combination of commitment with enthusiasm; it is the gift of the young. Psalm 8 is a hymn that celebrates God's glory and the God-given dignity of human beings. This includes children who speak 'out of the mouths of babes'. Children are not secondary to God's plan; they are good examples of his engagement with the world. David is singled out in preference to his older brothers and he is soon shown to be the better of his elders (1 Samuel 16.1–13). The high point of these themes is the messianic prophecy of the birth of Immanuel as told in Isaiah 7.14ff. The royal child is proclaimed who will re-establish justice and herald the kingdom of God. All this is the context within which Jesus would have understood the place of children. If God is so content to work through the young in this way, then the Church ought to be confident in sharing its most wonderful gift with pleasure. In journeying together, the faith can be taught to young and old alike.

The Gospel writers pull no punches about the importance of children. Jesus says 'I am the bread of life.' 'Whoever comes to me will never be hungry and whoever believes in me will never be thirsty.' The only inclusion criteria are to come and to believe, to 'believe and trust' as the baptism service says. Children offer this enthusiasm and this innocence that adults, especially in the Gospels, seem to have lost. At the feeding of the five thousand, with all its eucharistic overtones, it is a boy who provides the raw material for the miracle and the adults who provide the doubt. Matthew and Luke consider it important enough to record that the incarnation came through the birth of a child in ordinary circumstances and that this coming tells us something about God himself. Society often asks children to behave like adults: in the gospel of Jesus Christ we are asked to become like children in order to enter the kingdom of God.

Jesus is referred to at confirmation age in Luke 2.41–52. He is shown as being independent of his parents and confident among the teachers of the Temple. This is the only information in the Bible on Jesus' maturing. Quite apart from the wonder of his wisdom, the reason he is not missed at first by his parents is because of their trust in the community. Jewish community life and the high value placed on the family mean that his parents assume him to be with their friends and wider fellowship. Of course this young person is actually happy in the fellowship of faith set in God's house. In modern day Judaism, bar mitzvah takes place around the years twelve or thirteen and is the act of a boy taking personal responsibility to fulfil the Torah for himself within the community. Overtones with confirmation are obvious but there has been no separation from the worshipping life of the fellowship since circumcision. In Jesus, we are called into a new creation, and such distinctions should not exist. We are in this together whatever our age.

Three key texts show us ultimately how Jesus saw the place of children and young people.

The dispute about greatness (Mark 9.33–37, Matthew 18.1–5, Luke 9.46–48)

To be great in God's kingdom, one must be like an innocent child. The disciples have been arguing about their relative importance and status. We can all hear ourselves doing it: it is a common adult flaw. Competition is a given among adults. Jesus uses this tendency to teach his disciples about the importance of innocence and openness. More than this even, Jesus is showing us that there is still something in children that tells us about the nature of God himself. We lose this when we become adults, as the story of Adam and Eve so clearly represents. We are not challenged to become child-ish but child-like. For adults this requires a change of heart and mind.

Stumbling blocks (Mark 9.42, Matthew 18.6–7, Luke 17.1–2)

Jesus now goes further; there is a penalty to pay for getting in the way of these 'little ones'. If we are to be disciples, we need to take seriously Jesus' teaching and ensure, especially in the Church, that our systems and programmes do not get in the way. There is an important lesson here for the Church and the administration of confirmation. If you go to Capernaum on the shores of the Sea of Galilee, there are millstones on display from the time of Jesus. The connection between the penalty of the millstone and the adjacent sea would not have been lost on

Jesus' hearers. His words leave no room for doubt. We must beware that the churches in which we are placed do not become stumbling blocks for the young, the learning or the innocent.

Let the children come to me (Mark 10.13–16, Matthew 19.13–15, Luke 18.15–17)
Jesus is at least indignant if not angry in these passages, which reminds us of his anger at the cleansing of the Temple. The adults were actually getting in the way and stopping the children and young people from reaching Jesus. It is not just that they are young, but they know their dependence on God, their friendship with him, and all need to show these characteristics of the kingdom.

Journey food for all

It is clear from this summary that children have their place in the kingdom and grow in faith alongside adults. Instruction is something for all, all the time. In the Old Testament it is clear that children are the hope of God's future and that we are all God's children. In the New Testament Christ has shown us a model of discipleship to keep us all that little bit younger. There are no rules or hurdles to jump. We travel together and in company with each other in faith. To withhold baptized children from sharing in Christ through Holy Communion because of a confirmation still to come is not the revelation given to us through Scripture. To continue to grow in Christ with a moment of commitment on maturity – like confirmation – is natural and good. But we should travel together, sustained by the food for the journey, Christ himself.

The earliest Christians called their faith 'The Way'. This was how they articulated their response to living in a new way but also being on a journey of faith together. There is of course no explicit mention of children and young people sharing in the Eucharist in the New Testament. But the New Testament Church understood 'The Way' to be open to all and sharing in the Eucharist was not determined by age or status but by baptism. Families and households were baptized and initiated into the faith together (Colossians 3 and Ephesians 5). For many of these new Christians, those with Jewish roots in particular, this priority of including children was natural as they held a strong role in the Passover rituals. Jesus himself would have been brought up in this tradition. So as the worship of the early Church developed, mostly at first in people's homes, the sharing of communion among all the baptized would have been normal.

Similarly, there is no explicit evidence in the post-apostolic era that children and young people receiving communion was seen as a problem for the early Church. Infant baptism and communion were well established in Carthage by the time of Cyprian (d. 259). This ancient practice continues in the Orthodox Church to this day. In the fourth century the Apostolic Constitutions provide that children receive communion after the clergy, widows and deaconesses, but before the main body of adults. It was Augustine of Hippo who first made the theological link between baptism and participation in heaven through the doctrine of original sin. To deny children baptism by reason of age or lack of understanding was to deny them Christ himself in the form of bread and wine, their salvation. 'Unless you eat the flesh of the Son of Man and drink his blood, you have no life in you' (John 6.53). Infants should therefore be baptized as soon as possible and receive the outward signs of membership of the Church and full incorporation into Christ. These points had a special imperative when rates of infant mortality were so high.

In this context, developments followed as the Church grew in size and geographical spread. Bishops were there to baptize in the unified rite of baptism, confirmation and Eucharist. In time therefore, the water rite in baptism with the signing of the cross was increasingly delegated to presbyters and the bishop would 'confirm' this on his travels. The rite of confirmation began in this way but communion for the baptized was still the norm.

In the West, over a number of centuries, access to communion gradually decreased for the laity. Concerns over the administration of the consecrated elements, and an emphasis on 'attendance' at Mass rather than 'participation' became increasingly default positions. In 1281 Archbishop Peckham, at the Council of Lambeth, issued the regulation that those not confirmed (without good reason) should be barred from communion. Parents were neglecting to present their children to the bishop for the laying on of hands and so this was an attempt to turn back this indifference. The practice of communicating unconfirmed adults and children was finally abolished by the Council of Trent in the sixteenth century. At the Reformation and subsequently, the emphasis on instruction and understanding was promoted which compounded the prohibition of sharing communion with the unconfirmed. Cranmer's Prayer Book of 1662 stated: 'And there shall none be admitted to the Holy Communion until such time as he be confirmed or ready and desirous to be confirmed.' The pattern of Baptism followed much later by Confirmation and Communion is therefore a familiar pattern to members of the Church of England. However, at best it is a variation of ancient practice, and at worst, a stumbling block. The practice of other churches of administering communion at a much younger age and before confirmation, has largely remained and is more faithful to the apostolic tradition of the early Church.

The Parish Communion movement of the twentieth century did a lot to undo this puzzle of practice. The sense of gathering together to participate in the Eucharist as a baptized community encouraged the presence of children and young people, and their nurture. A series of significant church reports led the Church into a new understanding of the access of children to communion in relation to confirmation. In particular these reports changed thinking: *Children in the Way*, 1988, *All God's Children?*, 1991 and *On the Way – Towards an Integrated Approach to Christian Initiation*, 1994. In their book *Children, Churches and Christian Learning*,[2] Leslie J. Francis and Jeff Astley summarize the factors that, over this period of time, have come together to stimulate the debate and process towards admitting children to communion before confirmation. These factors are:

- the more central place of communion in the local church

- the move toward fuller participation by children in worship

- fresh discussion on the pattern of Christian initiation

- new understandings of how faith develops

- growing emphasis on the church as community

- fresh insights as to how children learn by participation

- demands both from children and parents for fuller participation

- recognition of changing practices ecumenically and internationally.

In 1996 the House of Bishops issued *Guidelines for Admission of Baptized Persons to Holy Communion before Confirmation,* and these 'guidelines' were subsequently accepted by the General Synod. Parishes began the process of re-discovery of sharing the Eucharist with all and resources were provided to enable change. In summary, the convincing arguments in favour of a change in practice seem to have been:

- the nature of baptism

- the acceptance of children in the church

- children's need for spiritual nourishment

- children's need to belong

- the need for adults to 'become as a child'.

The General Synod of the Church of England approved *Regulations for the Admission of Baptized Children to Holy Communion* in 2006 (GS 1596A).[3] Almost every diocese has its own advice for introducing this practice under the bishop's authority and permission, and resources are readily available to help parishes make this increasingly valued and important change.

Parishes and individuals often have questions and practical concerns regarding administration and these are discussed in detail in *Let the Children Come to Communion.*

Bells and whistles

To rethink confirmation requires a rethinking of communion before confirmation. The Church has successfully rediscovered this vital gift and can now move forward in confidence with all ages together. Without exception, those parishes that embrace communion before confirmation find this to be a liberating experience and the catalyst to changing for the better their mission outlook and nurture. Parishes that admit children to communion before confirmation grow.

Confirmation rethought-through is about affirming the value of personal commitment and discipleship which is then confirmed by the laying on of hands by the bishop. We are an episcopal church and the visit of the bishop signifies not only our fellowship with the rest of the Church but also our living heritage through the Spirit with the early Church and the inspiration of the Holy Spirit. Baptism may be all we need to be incorporated into Christ but the generosity of the Spirit is to be found in confirmation. Candidates really enjoy the rite of confirmation and the presence of the bishop says something that the local church cannot. Reconnecting with confirmation is about moving on from the 'passing out parade' and discovering the rich depths of maturity in the gospel faith.

At St Albans Cathedral we see this each year in a unique way. Diocesan confirmations come and go throughout the year but the Easter Confirmation is special. Any confirmation service in a cathedral is a great event as the bishop exercises his ministry in the place where his ministry is rooted, but at Easter St Albans has a different way of letting the candidates know that something has happened to them. We gather in the darkness of Holy Saturday evening and the salvation history recorded in Scripture is told – the creation, the flood, the exodus. We light the new fire and bring in the light of Christ as the Paschal Candle illuminates the vast Abbey. People come to the bishop for baptism and confirmation. As if to make our point in this book, the Eucharist is not celebrated, but candidates return to their parishes for the early morning celebration on Easter Day. The climax of the service is a unique and bizarre (only in St Albans!) proclamation of the resurrection. The whole congregation, led by the newly confirmed, gather before the high altar, and at the moment of the Alleluia, the organ sounds as loudly as it can and everyone makes a 'joyful noise', with hooters, bells, whistles, party poppers, foghorns, clapping and saucepans hit with wooden spoons (my personal favourite). It is slightly crazy, but as the din descends the majestic chords of the hymn 'Thine be the glory' sound out and we celebrate the resurrection. It's like a last night of the proms moment. The confirmed really know something has happened and their lives have changed forever. Many of them now have been fed by the sacrament for several years; this has been their coming of age. They never forget it and their faith in Jesus has been well and truly confirmed. They now fully belong.

Chapter 3

Adolescent Development and Confirmation

Pete Maidment

This chapter examines the different stages of adolescence and explores what confirmation might mean to a young person at each of these stages.

When writing about adolescent development (or actually any form of social science) it is helpful to start with a disclaimer. When using any kind of theory drawn from the social sciences you have to realize that you are dealing for the most part with generalizations. There is no such thing as one type of young person, that should be obvious to us all, and what the social sciences try to do is to say that, generally speaking, young people tend to behave in *this* way when faced with *that* situation. As soon as you have made a decision on what all young people are like you will find one who breaks that mould, and that should be no surprise. We are made by God, in his image, and we are each made unique. Young people, like the rest of us, refuse to be put in boxes.

However, it's also important to recognize that there are things to be learnt from the social sciences. Young people may not like being put into boxes but there are lots of things that we can say about them which, generally speaking, are true.

Therefore, please see each description included here as a generalized picture of young people at different stages of development. Try not to get too tied up with ages: all thirteen-year-olds are different (one of the many reasons why it would be wrong to ever say that at x age a young person is ready to be confirmed). Instead try to see the different stages of development and picture young people that you know and see if any of the theories apply to them. It's also worth noting that a young person may be at different levels of maturity according to which part of their make up you look at. Just because they are physically mature it doesn't necessarily mean that they are educationally mature: for example, a young person who is very mature in terms of their 'street cred', behaving in very adult ways in terms of how they present themselves and how they interact with people, may be spiritually very immature.

An introduction to adolescence

Adolescence, sociologist Louise J. Kaplan writes, is 'derived from the Latin root word *adolescere,* "to grow up," and is most often considered to be the period from puberty to adulthood or maturity'.[1] There was a time however when, quite simply, adolescence didn't exist. Children were children and then overnight they would become adults, whether by getting married, starting a job or an apprenticeship or through a ritual rite of passage such as the bar mitzvah for Jewish boys. Childhood would end and adulthood would begin. It is only really in the industrialized western world that adolescence has become any more than the moment at which a child becomes an adult.

Sociologists have been writing about adolescence since the start of the twentieth century but most of the key works date from the 1950s and 60s. One of the major thinkers in the field was the sociologist, Erik Erikson. In his seminal work *Childhood and Society,*[2] Erikson wrote about the different developmental stages or ages of the whole of human life, and included adolescence as a distinct developmental stage separate from childhood or young adulthood. Since then sociologists have broken adolescence down into ever more component parts, quickly realizing that the term was not broad enough to describe the great changes that mark the stepping off point from childhood to adulthood. In fact, whereas adolescence was originally viewed as the end of childhood we now view adolescence as the start of adulthood, and as a life phase that can take years to complete.

All change!

Essentially adolescence is a time of change. Everything changes!

Erikson called the period of adolescence the 'fidelity' stage explaining that it was during this stage of development that a child struggles to discover their own identity. A successful adolescence will result in an adult who knows their *identity* and an unsuccessful adolescence results in an adult who struggles with role *confusion*.[3] In other words, if the young person has a healthy adolescent stage in their life then they will come out the other end as an adult who has a good sense of who they are and what their role is, they will feel confident in their identity. Someone with a difficult or troubled adolescent period may well end up being quite unsure about their role and their identity, they will be left confused as to who they are meant to be and what their place in society is. Adolescence is where a person starts to ask questions like 'Who am I?', 'How do I fit in?' and 'Where am I going in life?'

Pete's reflection

In some aspects my adolescence was quite troubled. I grew up in a single parent family with a totally absent father (he had left when I was just three years old and I have had no contact with him since). While my mum did a wonderful job of raising me, the fact that I grew up with no father has had a profound effect on me in terms of discovering my identity. Typical of many young people who grew up in single parent families I struggle with self-confidence and tend towards a fairly low opinion of myself. I also find myself constantly looking for role models, for people to be pleased with what I have done. I think that if Erikson met me he would think me deeply confused!

A young person goes through all sorts of changes during adolescence. The most obvious of these is the physical changes that occur. In fact it is the biological changes that actually mark the beginning of adolescence. As a child enters puberty so they begin the journey of adolescence. This physical aspect of growing up appears to have remained stable for hundreds of years, and yet over the last 150 years children appear to be starting puberty earlier and earlier. Some biologists suggests that even 150 years ago the average age for girls beginning puberty was fourteen and a half; now the average in the US (according to a study by the Lifespan Health Research Center, Ohio) is twelve and a half with some scientists suggesting that the average may be as young as eleven and a half. So today young people are entering adolescence two years earlier than they would have 150 years ago. It is one of the reasons why it is so important for us to have a little bit of an understanding of adolescent development if we are to be able to prepare young people for confirmation at the right time.

As well as changing physically, a child also goes through a cognitive change during adolescence. The philosopher and developmental theorist Jean Piaget wrote at length about the cognitive development of children as they grow and develop.[4] Between the ages of eleven and fifteen Piaget argues the child develops an increasing ability to think in the abstract as well as in the real and is able to consider hypothetical matters. Whereas previously the child may only have been able to handle concrete concepts (things they can physically see and touch), by the time they reach the end of adolescence he or she should be able to engage in more sophisticated and elaborate information processing strategies, think about a problem from all sorts of different angles at the same time and to reflect about who they are and what they can do and achieve.[5]

Another change that occurs during adolescence is in where a young person finds their support. Until the start of adolescence a child finds their security almost exclusively from their family. Most pre-adolescents want to grow up to be like their mums or dads. They will often imitate their parents' behaviour and their beliefs. Sociologists Douglas C. Kimmel and Irving B. Weiner write that compared to an adolescent, a child has more cohesion with their mother and feels more accepted by their father; to the pre-adolescent child, mum and dad are everything and the process of adolescence puts those relationships under strain.[6] At this point it's important to note of course that our work will regularly bring us into contact with young people who do not have the secure family structure that they need. Many will be from single parent families and others will be in very difficult home settings. Working with these young people is vital as they are in such need of external support, support which the Church should be well positioned to offer. When you look at the importance of family to a young person from a developmental perspective, it is a stark reminder of how tough it is to grow up without that firm support.

Piaget asserts that while family should still provide an important system for children during adolescence, the peer group now enters their consciousness as an important place in which to find security and identity.

As young people gain more strength from their peer groups they naturally start to distance themselves from the support offered by their family networks. While this may sound unhealthy it is actually a normal and very formative part of adolescence. A young person now has the opportunity to make their own decisions, choose their own friends and friendship groups and form their own beliefs.[7]

The quest for individuation

So what is the purpose of adolescence? What do we hope that our young people will achieve through this long, painful, sometimes embarrassing and complicated life stage? 'The primary and most basic goal of adolescence is known as *individuation*', explains sociologist and theologian Chap Clark, and individuation essentially means 'becoming one's own person'.[8] Individuation, Clark continues, is the process by which a young person achieves 'identity, autonomy and reconnection'. It is difficult to explain individuation without writing several hundred words, but it is an important term to get to grips with if we are to understand what happens during adolescence. In order to become an adult we need to break away from what it means to be a child. A mature person is someone who has a healthy sense of identity, someone who has a strong sense of self. Individuation is the process by which we leave behind the childish way of finding our identity in (usually) our family and begin to explore who we are in relation to those around us. Individuation is the process of becoming a unique person.

At the same time, it's important to note what individuation isn't. An individuated person isn't an independent person. Independence isn't a sign of maturity. Individuation is closer to *inter*dependence. Interdependence, rather than saying 'I can do this by myself and I don't need any help' says 'I can do this because of who I am and who I have around me, I don't need to do this by myself because I have a community around me which can assist me.' A series of TV adverts from Orange did a good job of explaining interdependence. They each showed a montage of people who had helped someone become who they are. The tagline 'I am who I am because of everyone' is a very neat summing up of what it means to have a mature view of one's place with a society.

Psychologists John Conger and Nancy Galambos wrote that 'People who have achieved a strong sense of identity, especially after a period of active searching, are more likely to be more autonomous, creative and complex in their thinking; more open, less self-conscious, and less self-absorbed; and more resistant to pressure for conformity than adolescents who have not achieved a clear sense of identity.'[9] I don't know about you but that sounds like a brilliant description of what I'd like to see in a mature young person willing to stand up and be confirmed. Otherwise, if we confirm young people who are yet to start their quest for individuation then, by Conger's and Galambos's definition, we will be confirming young people who are dependent, unimaginative and simple in their thinking, closed, self-conscious, and self absorbed, and unable to resist pressure to conform. And while Conger and Galambos are keen to note that children start to develop an identity during early childhood they agree with Clark that the search for identity is most obvious during adolescence.

It is important to note here that we are not calling into question the innate spirituality of a child. Writers like Rebecca Nye in *The Spirit of the Child*[10] and Kathryn Copsey in *From the Ground Up* have done wonderful work in drawing to our attention the fact that a child is born fully spiritual. Kathryn Copsey writes '. . . we have before us the child created in the image of God, a deep spiritual being, gifted by God with qualities of openness, awareness, sensitivity, joy, trust, imagination and honesty'.[11] What develops around that spirituality is the child's faith. In an article entitled 'Spirituality and Children', Ruth White, Youth and Children's Work Training Development Officer for the Wessex Synod of the United Reformed Church writes 'We need to recognize that there is a dynamic relationship between religion/faith and spirituality, I think about faith being the scaffolding that gives shape to our spirituality . . .'[12] In pre-adolescent children that faith is generally inherited from their parents. The scaffolding might be strong but it's not necessarily something that they have built themselves. As the child passes through adolescence and gains a greater understanding of their own identity then they start to rebuild the scaffolding for themselves, borrowing from their parents' faith, but starting to add in what they are taught by others, the beliefs of their peers and of course what they work out for themselves.

The tightrope of adolescence

We've looked briefly at what happens during adolescence and at the overall 'purpose' (for the want of a better word) of this developmental stage – so the next question has to be 'When should we confirm our young people?'

Now, this is dangerous territory. The temptation is to try to lay down the law here, to draw a line in the sand and say that *this* is the age at which we should confirm and give all of the reasons for this. And while that is really tempting, it would also be fabulously unhelpful. We would instantly alienate everyone who confirms at a different age, and as noted earlier whenever you try to overgeneralize and say that all young people at this particular age are in this position you'll be barraged with examples of young people who don't fit the bill.

We've already looked at some things Chap Clark wrote in the great book *Starting Right*, but I want to give over the next few pages entirely to a picture he uses to illustrate the adolescence journey, the quest for individuation if you like. And it's always good to use pictures.

Picture, if you will, a tightrope in a big top. Perhaps you've been to the circus and seen someone on the high wire, or heard the story of Blondin as he walked across Niagara Falls on his tightrope.[13] Adolescence, Chap Clark says, is a bit like walking a tightrope and the analogy works on a couple of levels. First, it's tricky. I've never attempted a tightrope walk but I know that there's a good deal involved in staying up there on the wire and not plummeting to the ground, you've got to balance and concentrate and not be scared and not look down and . . . actually that's as far as my knowledge of tightrope walking goes.

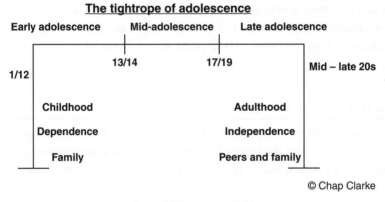

The tightrope of adolescence

Early adolescence	Mid-adolescence	Late adolescence
	13/14	17/19
1/12		Mid – late 20s
Childhood		Adulthood
Dependence		Independence
Family		Peers and family

© Chap Clarke

Chap Clarke's Tightrope of adolescence[14]

We've already discussed that moving through the adolescent life span is equally complex.

The other thing that I know about tightrope walking is that it would be impossible without the two stanchions at either end of the rope. Chap

Clark suggests that in the journey of adolescence the stanchions represent the two sources of support that a child moves between. At one end of the rope, the major source of support is the family structure. At the other end is individuation, the point where the child knows their place and their role in culture and in society and is able to choose for themself where they find their support.

Along the way Chap Clark divides adolescence into three clear categories: pre-adolescence, mid-adolescence and late adolescence. In the next section of this chapter, we're going to explore each of these stages and then imagine what a child at that stage might look like in terms of behaviour, understanding and character. We'll then look at some of the reasons why this might be a good time to confirm and some of the reasons why it might be a bad time to confirm.

Pre-adolescence

It's worth starting just to the left of the tightrope and remembering that up until this point the child has been a child. Throughout the first eleven or twelve years of life a child's sense of self is grounded in familial relationships. It's also true that any child is striving for independence from the moment it is born: any parent who has been through the daily struggle of trying to dress a toddler will know this to be true instinctively, and I'm sure that my daughter isn't the only child who after mastering 'mama' and 'dada' almost immediately followed them with 'no' or to be more accurate, 'NO, NO, NO, aaaaaarghhh!' Kimmel and Weiner write that during the primary school years children expand their knowledge of the world and learn ways of managing their experiences that make them increasingly self-reliant and less in need of supervision, ideally within the safe bounds of the family. It is healthy to teach pre-adolescent children about Christian faith, and to help them to get on that discipleship journey. We feel that it's also healthy, if it is the custom of your church, to encourage a child at this stage to make a personal commitment to Jesus Christ and to partake in the Eucharist because it is a part of what the family do, or because the family have allowed it. We are also free to help them learn how to pray and to read the Bible and to share their faith.

Furthermore, we can learn a huge amount about God and the Christian faith from children of this age. In Mark 10 Jesus is quite explicit about the child's place in the kingdom:'. . . the kingdom of God belongs to such as these. I tell you the truth, anyone who will not receive the kingdom of God like a little child will never enter it' he indignantly tells the disciples when they try to shoo the children and their mothers away from him.

And yet we need to bear in mind, with what we know about development of children and where a child finds his or her identity at this age, that their faith is most likely to be based on or imitated from that of their parents, and while that doesn't mean it is any less faith than an adult's, it does mean that it has yet to be tested in the fires of adolescence and is yet to be fully owned by that child. It's also worth remembering that plenty of children who seem to have a strong or rich faith in their childhood or even early teens quickly drop or lose that faith as they progress through adolescence. Our experience in visiting churches is that by the age of ten or eleven attendance at groups has started to drop. Even churches with thriving children's work can struggle to keep young people attending once they get to secondary school age.

A child confirmed in pre-adolescence is likely to be in what psychologist James Marcia calls the 'diffusion stage' of development.[15] Meredith Miller and Kara Powell from Fuller Youth Institute describe the characteristics of the diffusion stage thus: 'This status can be understood as the "don't know, don't care" status. This stage describes adolescents who have not experienced an identity "crisis" or even done any exploration, nor do they have a stable set of commitments. Persons in diffusion have simply not thought about their identity. They are not sure what they believe about key issues such as religion, politics, gender roles, or occupation, nor are they concerned with them.'[16]

A child in the diffusion stage of development would make a great confirmation candidate in some ways, in that she would be keen to please, she wouldn't want to question any part of the Christian faith or the promises she was being asked to make, simply because it wouldn't have occurred to her to question them. And that is really the problem with confirming a child at this stage: it could be simply another activity along with learning to play the flute and going to the cinema. It is possible that there would not be any depth to the decision.

Early adolescence

We used to run an open youth club for eleven- to fourteen-year olds on Friday nights at the church where I was the youth worker. One of the girls, Gemma,[17] was a regular. She was in the first year of the club so she was eleven years old (year 7 at school). She usually turned up wearing the same as the other girls of her age – often something pink. One night, however, she turned up decked head to toe in black, sporting the full Goth ensemble. I was a little bemused as this seemed such a drastic overnight change and I couldn't really work out what had happened. Then at the end of the night I got my answer when Gemma's big sister turned up to walk her home: she too was decked out in full Goth gear. Gemma was clearly wearing Goth cast offs. Brilliant! As the weeks progressed Gemma still wore bits and bobs from her Goth ensemble, but it was toned down; that first week she was simply trying out a new identity.

Back to the tightrope. At the early adolescence stage the child has climbed the stanchion and is taking the first tentative steps into adolescence. If we're agreed that adolescence begins in biology then this child has begun puberty and, whether they like it or not, adulthood is beckoning.

Chap Clark writes that 'young adolescents have just begun to ask the question of identity. The identity of a young adolescent is still firmly fixed within the contexts of the family system, although the child will at times struggle to try on new identities, even at this early stage.'[18]

Whenever I have run confirmation classes for children at this stage of development, what has struck me most has been their eagerness. Every question asked is greeted with a forest of hands and a chorus of 'Ooh, ooh, ask me! Ask me! I know, I know!' Rather than trying to listen and understand and develop in their faith these young people were just desperate to show their knowledge in order to impress. Just like the children in the diffusion stage of adolescent development, they were marked out by their eagerness and their desire to conform.

Marcia described this stage of adolescence as the 'foreclosure stage', which Miller and Powell sum up like this: 'This is a status in which adolescents have definite opinions about their identity, but those opinions have been inherited from external forces rather than cultivated from within themselves. They have stable commitments, but have not experienced exploration or crisis. For example, they vote how their parents vote, not because they have chosen to agree with their parents, but because they have never questioned the political views they inherited.'[19]

The early adolescents in my confirmation class were simply answering the questions as their parents (or more worryingly I) had taught them to answer. They didn't question anything because they weren't really concerned; they had been given the answers and that was all they needed. Erikson would have argued that these young people had never faced any crisis in which to test their faith and so they were only able to rely on the faith of others.

In a similar way to young people in the diffusion stage of development, young people who are going through foreclosure make great confirmation candidates – they're really easy to teach (provided you can get them to sit still for long enough) and they'll agree with everything you say. They'll turn up to confirmation bright-eyed and bushy-tailed and grin encouragingly at the bishop. It doesn't matter how many times you say that they don't have to get confirmed unless they really feel ready, they will still smile broadly at you and affirm that, yes, of course they want to go through with it and why do you keep asking such silly questions?

The trouble as before is that while it may appear that they have made a true and genuine decision to stand up and be counted, for the vast majority of these early adolescents the decision will still be based on what they feel their family want them to do. Kimmel and Weiner make two quite alarming observations of this group. First, they note that 'adults . . . are likely to praise foreclosed adolescents for their reliability, steadfastness and sense of purpose' while acknowledging that young people in the foreclosure stage of adolescent development tend to make 'premature personal commitments as a way of skirting exploration and avoiding uncertainty'.[20]

Mid-adolescence

While working at the church where I met Gemma the Goth, I regularly took RE lessons in the local secondary school. At one point I was asked to lead a lesson on life after death for two classes at two different ages. The class, who were year 8 (i.e. age twelve to thirteen), typically early adolescents in the foreclosure stage of development, went along very comfortably with what I taught. I had planned an hour of teaching, and easily fitted all of the activities, illustrations, stories and questions into the allocated time. When I did the exact same lesson for a year 10 group (i.e. age fourteen to fifteen), typically mid-adolescents, the response was completely different. In that lesson I didn't manage to get through more than the first fifteen minutes of what I had planned before the quizzing began, and the rest of our time together was filled with trying to field dozens of questions. In each lesson I asked what the young people believed would happen to them if they were to die. In the younger class there were very well-defined answers, such as 'I would go to heaven', 'I would just cease to exist' and so on – typical of what I would have expected from young people at the foreclosure stage. They had answers that they had picked up and it hadn't occurred to them to question them, someone had told them this was the truth and so they were content to accept it. The older class came up with much more typical answers for young people in mid-adolescence: 'I don't really know', 'It depends', 'How can we tell?'

They were leaving the stage of their development where they were happy with concrete answers and were starting to explore more abstract concepts. They were no longer content simply to accept what they had been told and rather wanted to work things out for themselves, to discuss and explore.

Going back to Chap Clark's tightrope illustration, things are now starting to get a bit scary. The young people have headed out into the middle of the rope – they've had to let go of the first stanchion, the strength and security that comes from relying on their family for their identity, but they are yet to grab hold of anything more substantial for support. The family are still very much present and, in times of crisis, the young person is likely to rush back to that safety area, but they are unlikely to admit that their family remains as a place of security for them.

Marcia calls this period of adolescence the 'moratorium phase'. Powell and Miller sum it up like this: 'the moratorium status is the stage in which individuals challenge what they have inherited. They question who they are and what they believe and are unable to land on clearly defined beliefs and standards. This is the stage in which individuals challenge what they have inherited. For this reason they will often express doubts and uncertainties about what they believe.'[21]

Clark reckons that if you ask a young person in the foreclosure status of their development if they have any doubts about their religious beliefs you will get an answer something along the lines of 'No, not really, our family is pretty much in agreement on these things.' A young person in the moratorium status, however, will answer the same question in this kind of way, 'Yeah I guess I'm going through that now. I just don't see how there can be a God and yet so much evil in the world.'[22]

Young people in the moratorium stage are likely to show signs of uncertainty and insecurity, they will need loads of support, remember they're in the middle of the tightrope, they've got nothing to hold on to. Arguably, it is at this stage that our work with young people is the most vital: a youth leader or clergyperson can provide an enormous amount of stability throughout this phase. He or she can journey alongside the young person and hold their hand, helping them to keep taking tentative steps forward while, in the ideal world, always helping them to stay close to their family. In instances where adolescents do not have the luxury of a family to fall back on, our support needs to be doubled, as well as ensuring that we work closely with whichever authorities have been tasked with the young person's care.

What leaders must not do, but often fall foul of, is to try and force young people back to the foreclosure status. Adults, and particularly parents, may get an awful lot of security if children have strong solid opinions, and appear to agree with them and mimic their behaviour. To encourage young people's questioning and searching can be really quite scary – what if they choose to disagree with us?

To push young people back to foreclosure though would be disastrous, unless we want grown adults to remain at home with their parents well into their 40s and 50s (the example of Timothy in the 1980s sitcom *Sorry* comes to mind). The point is that just like teaching a child to ride a bike, at some point we have to let them go. While giving children all the support we can, we also need to allow them to take off under their own steam. It *is* scary (the first time I rode a bike without stabilizers I cycled straight into a ten-foot-high pile of railway sleepers), but it is also vital in helping the young person develop a right sense of identity, and in giving them the best opportunity of becoming a fully individuated adult.

So what about confirmation – does a mid-adolescent make a good confirmation candidate? This is a really tricky one. On one level mid-adolescence is a great time for confirmation preparation, provided we are happy for the young people to set the agenda. They will be full of questions and doubts, and we will need to give them lots of time and space to explore and unpack all of those insecurities and concerns. At this stage they are likely to shy away from definites: they will want to be working things out for themselves rather than be given all the answers. It is possible that by forcing a young person through confirmation at this stage we actually force them backwards in their development. On the other hand, it seems likely that it is at this stage that the young person is most likely to drift away from the church or from their faith. If they are full of questions but find no one in the church to help them with the answers then they will search elsewhere.

I remember working with a young person who discovered this moment of moratorium quite suddenly and starkly. She was a very high achiever, gaining top marks in pretty much every exam that she took both at GCSE and A-Level. She was all set to go to medical school to study to become a doctor. She was the shining light in our youth work, seemingly full of faith, and confidence; a real leader. I can remember quite vividly the day when she came to me in genuine shock and panic. I thought that something really serious had happened so palpable was her shock. I asked her what the problem was and she explained that she had suddenly realized that her faith wasn't her own: even at the age of seventeen to eighteen she was still living on her parents' faith, the expectations of her church, and actually that was no good. She had suddenly realized that she had to own this stuff for herself; unless she could examine her faith and God and find out whether or not they measured up for her personally then she felt she had missed the point. She was terrified that because she had all of these questions and all of these doubts in something that she had grown up knowing to be true, and indeed had been confirmed in at the age of twelve, then her faith must be a sham. It was a real privilege to be able to stand alongside this girl as she asked her questions and to assure her that there was nothing wrong with doubts, nothing wrong with questions – that actually it was perfectly normal and perfectly healthy to go through this stage. What an honour for a youth worker or any other adult to be the person who helps guide a young person through that tricky moratorium phase of their life.

So whether we choose to confirm young people at this point or not, one thing is certain: we will need to accompany them and walk with them through this part of their development, we need to listen and not judge, we need to be a source of strength and security, and all of this, whenever possible, in *partnership* with the young person's family.

Late adolescence

Late adolescence, traditionally speaking, is the final stepping off point of the adolescent development process. It is the far end of the tightrope where the young person is able to step out of the insecurity and uncertainty of the bouncy middle portion, on to the final stanchion. This is where the young person has reached the point of individuation, an ability to recognize their position in society and to be able to have confidence in their own identity; to be able to put their security in who they are in relation to their family, their peers and their culture. Marcia calls this stage of adolescence 'achievement': 'the goal of identity development is to reach the achieved status. It is the status wherein individuals have explored who they are and what they believe and hold stable commitments to a set of beliefs, values and standards. Their identity is defined, and they have thought through their perspectives',[23] explain Miller and Powell.

There are two clear points to understand about this status of adolescent development. First, that according to Marcia the achievement moment of development should be just that, a moment. In other words, whereas all the other statuses are clearly periods of time through which an adolescent moves, this final moment is when the young person achieves individuation. They struggle through the moratorium period questioning and seeking and exploring what it means to be in individual, to achieve their own identity and then as adolescence draws to an end, adulthood begins. Maturity has been achieved.

The second point is that the first point clearly no longer applies.

Faith development is just one aspect of identity formation; during moratorium a young person explores everything about who they are, from their sexual orientation to the career they want to pursue. Someone who is in the moratorium stage of development will want to experiment and test out everything, every kind of lifestyle and every kind of identity, and don't those fine chaps in the advertising world know it!

And so our consumer culture encourages us to experiment and test and try and buy . . . And it says don't grow up because then you'll have to stop having all this fun . . . And be responsible and discover who you are, and that will mean settling down into one identity, and that means you'll spend less money, and that means the ad man will be out of a job.

Historically, as we have already noted, adolescence ended with a rite of passage, an induction into the adult world. But today there isn't any clear rite of passage for young people to use as their stepping off point into adulthood; rather, as Kimmel and Weiner explain, we have dozens of mini rites, for example, playing the lottery, riding a moped, leaving school, having sex, getting married at sixteen, driving a car at seventeen, buying cigarettes and voting at eighteen . . . a whole succession of little moments marking out the boundaries of adulthood, and the result, sadly, is utter confusion. Ask a young person at what age they will become an adult and you'll be greeted with bafflement, or maybe even anger 'I don't ever want to be an adult!'

Psychologist Peter Blos writes that prolonged adolescence occurs when adolescence, 'a developmental phase which is intended to be left behind after it has accomplished its task; has become a way of life'.[24] In sociological terms (and I'm aware how this sounds) it's the problems caused when an adult would rather continue indulging in typical adolescent behaviour than take on the maturity and responsibility that comes with becoming an adult and discovering one's own identity, or more simply when an adult refuses to grow up.

While prolonged adolescence continues to be quite a hotly debated topic among sociologists and psychologists, there can be no doubt that in the industrialized West we have pretty much lost any kind of rite of passage. Instead we have allowed the process of becoming an adult to become confused. Many major sociologists who write on adolescent development are keen to point out that it must end at some point. For example, Richard Marohn writes of adolescence ending when the young adult has chosen the vocation, companions and avenues through which he will express his values and ideals.[25] Chap Clark is very clear that the tightrope must end. That final stanchion is there for a purpose, to mark the point at which adolescence finishes and adulthood begins.

If only there was a rite of passage; a celebration, if you like, to help mark the end of childhood and a step into adulthood. If only we could think of something we could do to help young people celebrate becoming an adult.

It's fairly obvious what we're getting at. In the Anglican Church we have a wonderful way to join with young people in celebrating becoming an adult, to 'put childish ways behind me' as Paul writes in 1 Corinthians.

If the Church wants to be able to assist young people in their adolescence then it seems sensible that we draw alongside them as they go through the tumultuous mid-adolescent, moratorium stage of development and offer confirmation as the rite of passage that will mark their coming of age in the Church's eyes. We'll look at ways of helping young people take up adult roles in our churches in Chapter 7.

A final disclaimer

Before drawing this chapter to a complete close it may be worth revisiting the disclaimer that I shared at the opening. Many of you will have found this chapter deeply frustrating – some because it didn't seem to describe the young people that you work with, and some because you don't really want to be viewed as a grown-up either and so it is a bit painful to read about prolonged adolescence. Others may have struggled with the concept that the beginning of adulthood may mark the end of development. I can empathize with all those struggles!

Richard Marohn concludes his paper on prolonged adolescent thus: '. . . to continue to hold that successful adolescent development must eventuate in a relatively inflexible organization of drives and defences blinds us to healthy manifestations of the adolescent period and to the continuous nature of development in adulthood.' In other words, there is nothing wrong with adolescence: it isn't a nasty part of life that we need to get young people through as quickly as possible, it's nothing to be embarrassed about and it's nothing to be ashamed of. All that stress and worry and change and confusion is all part of developing an identity. In a funny way we should relish it – it's the time in our lives when more than any other we get to form who we are and who we will be. That doesn't mean that development stops the moment we grow up either! It slows down certainly, we have fewer new experiences and become more defined the older we get, but we don't ever stop changing and developing, it's just that (thankfully) those changes come a little slower giving us plenty more time to reflect on each change and to worship the God who stays constant throughout.

Chapter 4

Faith Development and Confirmation

Susie Mapledoram

When I was little I had a small tub of soil on the window ledge of our kitchen. It contained a very generous quantity of cress seeds and each day I would come downstairs, inspect my very small vegetable patch and feel despondent that there was no sign of cress. And as often as my parents would remind me of patience and the science of plant growth, I became frustrated by no signs of development. Frankly, I didn't care how it happened, I just wanted cress. Waiting wasn't an option and I slowly lost interest. And when the cress eventually appeared a couple of weeks later, I wasn't that bothered and I had already cheated and got some cress from the local supermarket. Understanding the process wasn't something I took much interest in, I just wanted results and those results would take the form of . . . cress.

Let's be clear, this isn't a chapter on growing small vegetables, but I am convinced that had I taken time to understand how my cress grew and the stages it went through, I might have had a different perspective on my horticultural aspirations. This chapter is an opportunity to explore two faith development theories and see how they might inform how we approach our opportunities to accompany and support young people through their confirmation preparation, the service itself and what happens afterwards, recognizing that this is part of their ongoing discipleship. They don't necessarily fit snugly into our own experiences, but they bring some insights worth sharing.

Let's start with a true story.

When I was about twelve I was given the opportunity to be confirmed. I clearly remember feeling that this was a sign – a sign that I had been chosen, a sign that I had obviously reached strategic heights in holiness and spiritual fervour and a sign that I could be presented to the rest of the church as a proper Christian who understood that the answers to all questions at our Sunday school were likely to be 'Jesus' (97 per cent) or 'me' (3 per cent).

My confirmation classes began – oh happy days! Yes, I liked the curate who ran them. I got a free book and squash (that was quite something in those days). I got to go shopping with my mum to buy a tasteful outfit for the day. I started to think of exciting confirmation gifts I might get, including a free bookmark from the church (again, that wasn't to be sniffed at). But, the fundamental and life-changing reason for getting confirmed, what drove me each week to give my all to the classes, what compelled me to think through the service in detail was the fact that I had a totally life-absorbing crush on a boy in my church confirmation class. His name was Toby. I was completely in love and if I stood a chance of capturing his heart then I had to get confirmed. Oh yes, and I think I sort of believed that God was hanging around somewhere and he was quite nice and could be relevant to the process.

Other people had made the decision that it would be good for me to get confirmed and I went with the flow. I don't really remember much about the service (apart from Toby, of course) and I don't recall any significant changes in my life. I made huge promises and declarations of faith when I had really no idea what my faith was about. I began my life as a 'full' member of the Church, taking communion but not paying any attention to the huge symbolism within the bread and wine.

This is just one case study of one young person who got confirmed too soon. I was going through a faith rite of passage that confronted me with questions I didn't understand and beliefs that weren't important to me – and yet somewhere it was decided that I would be ready at this stage of my faith. I was either a very good spiritual actress or someone was getting commission on confirmation numbers – undoubtedly it was the first. But this raises again the question of when we confirm our young people. Is their readiness for the rite something that we determine or they decide?

In this chapter we are going to explore the nature of faith development, tiptoe through two of the more commonly used faith development theories, and discuss how they might be useful in our ministry with young people and specifically how we weave confirmation into their ongoing discipleship and as a rite of faith passage.

I'm aware that some of those reading this chapter will have explored the works of Westerhoff and Fowler, reflected on their theories and come to their own conclusions. I've had conversations with a number of people who have criticisms of these theories and see gaping holes in their ideas, so let me make it clear that we aren't putting all our eggs in their faith development theory baskets, but using their structures as a way of highlighting how young people's faith development could be perceived.

The analogy of journey is one of the most used in many a youth club talk or Sunday morning sermon. It's a picture that we can all relate to even if it's thinking about the walk to church or a ten-hour flight you may still be recovering from – we know beginnings, durations and ends. It's a hugely helpful analogy used a number of times in the Bible – for example the story of the two men walking from Jerusalem to Emmaus. They were weighing up the events of recent days when they were joined by someone who answered their questions with wisdom, insight and revelation and who, at the end of their journey, revealed himself as the risen Messiah. Those two men would never forget that physical journey because of the spiritual journey that ran in parallel with it. The well-known image from Hebrews of running the race with perseverance, looking to Jesus the author and perfector of our faith, understanding that the sin that weighs us down affects our aero-dynamics and being inspired by the Old Testament stories of faith warriors have been the source of encouragement and challenge for many as they have travelled their journey of faith.

American youth ministry expert and author, Duffy Robbins recalls a number of writers from the Middle Ages who talk about pilgrimages and journeys in his book, *This Way to Youth Ministry*. He goes on to quote Alister McGrath, who introduces the Latin word 'viator', meaning 'wayfarer or traveller' and how that has inspired many not just to talk about the journey but to make pilgrimages and learn from them.[1] The faith development theories of both Fowler and Westerhoff have a structure of stages throughout life and are helpfully or unhelpfully loosely aligned to a specific age range. Fowler claims that:

> Faith is interactive and social; it requires community, language, ritual and nurture. Faith is also shaped by initiatives from beyond us and other people, initiatives of spirit and grace. How these latter initiatives are recognized and imaged, or unperceived and ignored, powerfully affects the shape of faith in our lives[2]

Westerhoff's theories around faith are again active. He states that 'faith is a way of behaving which involves knowing, being and willing . . . faith itself is something we do. Faith is an action. It results from our actions with others, it changes and expands through our actions with others, and it expresses itself daily in our actions with others.'[3]

However, a major distinction lies in how that faith develops; Fowler would suggest that his stages of development supersede each other as a deciduous tree loses leaves and regrows new ones, yet Westerhoff, through the analogy of rings in a tree trunk, would say that a new stage builds on the one before and ultimately all four stages remain.

As we look at the stages of faith that both these theorists suggest, you might find it helpful to link a young person in your church, youth group or school to these stages and reflect on whether the pattern connects with their lives and faith experiences or not. Please be assured that there are no right or wrong answers in this, but it's crucial that we don't squeeze our young people around and into structures that clearly don't fit and, even worse, decide on their readiness for confirmation on that basis.

Fowler's stages of faith development

Stage One: Intuitive – Projective (4 to 8 years)
The child collects images of faith from people around them such as parents, teachers and other significant adults

Stage Two: Mythic – Literal (6–7 to 11–12 years)
The child begins to figure out the difference between what is real and what is fictional or fantasy. They begin to understand elements of the nature of God in that he is faithful and begin to connect themselves to him and hence find security in it.

Stage Three: Synthetic – Conventional (12 years to adult)
This is all about the interpersonal. The young person establishes different roles around different people and situations. They may act differently at youth group or at church, to the way they act around their peers at school or college. Very like Westerhoff's theory, this stage embraces the importance of being part of a peer group and the recognition for both the young person and the group of belonging.

Stage Four: Individuative – Reflective (young person and onwards)
This is the stage, Fowler suggests, that the young person's faith becomes their own through a variety of processes including questioning, discussion and evaluation. Their faith becomes more about what they believe rather than what they have been told to believe or think they should believe.

Stage Five: Conjunctive (30s–40s and onwards)
This stage is where the person draws on the experiences of Stage Four and becomes aware of who God is and how limited their understanding and faith in him is. This stage creates the opportunity to build that faith through 'honest reflection and

> open dialogue to deepen understanding of faith and how it
> applies to real life' (Robbins, *The Way to Youth Ministry*).
>
> *Stage Six: Universalizing (mid-life and onwards)*
> The person has a total commitment to their faith and what it
> means, and therefore their life becomes an outworking of that
> commitment and fervour. This is a stage that very few people
> achieve. Many writers who have reflected on Fowler's theory of
> faith development agree that this is a stage that demands utter
> selflessness and a totally radical lifestyle.

We are now going to look more specifically at Westerhoff's stages of
faith development. His four stages offer us a chance to explore some
key areas of work with our young people in exploring faith and create
some interesting questions around confirmation.

Before we begin, it's helpful to know a bit more about Westerhoff's
theory. It comes from a church/Christian background, and these stages
of development have been criticized as being structured around those
who go to church from a young age. Questions have understandably
been asked, therefore about their applicability to those young people
who have joined youth groups and churches in their teenage years,
and these questions need to be borne in mind.

It is also useful to understand Westerhoff's analogy of the rings in
a tree trunk. The idea that the stages add onto each other and inform
each other, rather than disappearing when a new stage is entered, is a
useful and challenging picture for me as a Christian and as a youth
worker.

I remember when I was at junior school there was a huge kudos
around which number maths book or reading book you were on, and
if you went up a colour stage in the reading books it was a time of
monumental celebration. It marked the beginning of a new stage, a
new reading era and another level up the ladder of reading genius. But

if it all went wrong and the new book proved to be too difficult (for me this happened regularly in maths), the thought of going back to the previous book was just unthinkable. As leaders, we are understandably keen for our young people to grow and develop, to come to an understanding of the gospel, Bible teachings and the foundations of the Christian faith. So when the situation arises when one of our young people 'seems' to back-pedal and land back at the first square of the spiritual snakes and ladders board we can feel a variety of emotions from frustration to guilt to disappointment. The thought of moving on to a new stage, having completed the previous stage of faith development and leaving what is behind is great. But what we leave behind is formational and foundational to where we are now. Sometimes we need to revisit, in story and testimony, those foundational stages to remind ourselves of who we are and why we do what we do. If, however, that stage has lost its importance by being superseded, then we may well cultivate an attitude that previous stages have lost their value and significance to us. So much of what we do in working with young people concerns stories and testimony, retelling the journey that we and they have taken through those previous stages, and we know ourselves the powerful impact they have on their lives and on ours also.

In his book, *Will Our Children Have Faith?*,[4] Westerhoff draws other pertinent analogies to trees that support his stages. For example, he states that trees only grow in a good environment – a strong element of how we develop faith is through experiences and interactions with others and if we don't have those around us it can restrict us from growing to our full potential.

I've never seen a tree grow overnight or even in a couple of weeks but I've walked through familiar parks and driven down local roads and noticed that what was once small is now big. I've even had the privilege of standing at the foot of a massive Canadian tree with a trunk as wide as three really wide houses and a top that disappears into the sky and wondered how many years it took to get to that place.

Westerhoff says 'a tree acquires one ring at a time in a slow and gradual manner. We do not see that expansion, although we do see the results, and surely we are aware that you cannot skip rings.' He is clear that we have to travel through these four stages, see the growth and that it is a gradual process.

Westerhoff's stages of faith development

> **Stage One: Experienced Faith (pre-school and childhood)**
>
> This is the stage where the child is discovering and experiencing faith. They will test, explore and react to all that's going on around them and tend to copy the ways of others.

It's a time to take role modelling seriously. How many times have I said something or done something that I didn't think would be noticed by a five-year-old godson? And, lo and behold, to my embarrassment it is recalled verbatim a few hours or days later. This stage is a challenge to us to be aware that the children we might be involved in working with are watching us.

If we are to roughly 'guestimate' an age range for this stage I would reckon on 0–9/10. By Westerhoff's theory the faith is there at an experiential level. Let's not underestimate the development that takes place here. He states: 'Experience is fundamental to faith. A person first learns Christ not as a theological affirmation, but as an affective experience.'[5] But I'm not sure that confirmation is an experience that should be included into this stage – you may think this is a given but I am aware of churches that are happy to confirm children as young as seven years old. Much of the experience that these children and young people encounter during this suggested stage will be what they see in others and it's the time that we might suggest that they begin to formalize someone else's faith as their own.

Stage Two: Affiliative Faith (adolescence)

Here Westerhoff suggests that the development of our faith is influenced by those people who journey with us. There is a strong sense of belonging to a group and being with others who are exploring similar faith journeys, as well as being positively affected by those who are part of their wider faith community (church).

If we were looking at these stages literally and measuring our work with young people against them, then we'd have a big tick in the youthwork box when it comes to the affliative stage. The need to belong and find a place within a group of similarly aged people is acute – 'where they know everyone's name and they are missed when absent. Of crucial importance is the sense that we are wanted, needed, accepted and important to the community'.[6] Taking place in the adolescent years and reflecting the importance of being in a group and journeying together in faith is clearly a justification that youthwork is a good idea.

This stage raises two points for me, well a point and a question.

If I were to align my own faith development with Westerhoff's stages then I would say that this is the stage were I was confirmed. It was a group thing (including, of course, the lovely Toby); we met together, we learnt together, we travelled together to the preparation classes and ultimately we were confirmed together. It was a shared experience. But, on reflection, I wonder if we were really a group that was confirmed as a unit, rather than as distinctive, faith-owning, individual young people. Was it the right time? No, I'm not sure it was. As a group we travelled that journey but within a matter of a couple of years that group naturally grew apart and being confirmed didn't seem to matter any more as it appeared to be a group experience rather than an individual one. I'm not suggesting that we shouldn't have prepared as a group, far from it, but I fear I took safety from the big faith questions in that group and merely fulfilled a criterion, rather than waited and made sure I understood I knew what I was agreeing to in that chilly cathedral.

That whole issue/question topples over into another thought around the affliative faith stage. Should we be thinking differently about how we prepare our young people for confirmation? We will be looking at this further in a more practical chapter later in the book, but should we be thinking innovatively around those confirmation classes we've always been running (more than likely in the vicar's lounge or vestry) and look at the need for affiliation but also at that individual need for a sense of belonging and being in that group. Losing young people from our churches after confirmation is sadly becoming more and more common and, in an attempt to address this, in a local church where I've worked we looked at the process of preparation and the ongoing youth work in the church. There would be two clearly distinct groups; those preparing for confirmation and those who were confirmed already. The preparation group had a beginning, middle and an end – the young people joined at the start of the preparation period, did all the sessions and the group ended essentially on the day of the confirmation service. The church worked very hard to integrate these young people into the 'post-confirmation' group, but this was a struggle and many of the newly confirmed young people just disappeared. We talked through the structure of the groups, the content of the evenings and how the confirmation preparation could be woven into the weekly evenings in a way that meant everyone was exploring the key themes whether they had been confirmed or not. And the most strategic change that the church made was to *ask the young people* when they felt that they were ready for confirmation. The young people are no longer part of a factory line process of preparation but woven into the ongoing ministry for young people in the church.

It's not an unusual story and it's a challenge to us all in how we prepare young people for confirmation. Maybe we have got into a system that from our perspective works. But are we merely making candidates or discipling young Christians?

> **Stage Three: Searching Faith (late adolescence)**
>
> Westerhoff suggests that this is the stage where older young people might begin to question and doubt all that they have learnt and explored about faith. It's a stage where they might explore other spiritualities and phenomena, but also a stage where they explore their faith more deeply and diferent ways in which they could express that faith.

This stage fascinates me the most and has had a powerful effect on my work with young people. This whole area of doubt and questioning can be seen by some as quite negative – we don't want young people to doubt God and all that he has done for them – but at the same time Westerhoff implies that this could be a very beneficial element of faith development that should inform our work with young people. Do we create space in our ministry, relationships, programmes with young people for them to question and doubt? I'm not suggesting that every Wednesday we have some kind of doubt and questioning confessional planned into our youth work, but when a young person approaches you and says 'I'm not sure anymore' – what is the nature of our response? Do we freak out, call the vicar, put them back through Sunday school or continue to accompany them on their journey of exploring faith by talking about their questions and remaining a consistent, loving advocate for them . . . and then confirm them?

'Typically . . . we have placed confirmation, which asks for a personal commitment of faith and a commitment to discipleship in the world, at the age when persons need to be encouraged to doubt, question and experiment . . . Perhaps confirmation should be moved to early adulthood and a new early adolescent rite celebrated on St Thomas' Day developed.'[7] Maybe, just maybe Westerhoff has a point here. Are we in so much of a rush to confirm our young people and of the belief that once they are confirmed they are 'spiritually sorted', that we don't allow them the space to ask those questions that buzz around their heads and speak of their doubts? Westerhoff goes on to suggest that our sometimes negative attitude to doubting and questioning could be linked to the fact that those very people who are preparing young people for confirmation themselves did not have the space to address their own wonderings and questions about faith. 'It appears, regretfully, that many adults in the church have never had the benefit of an environment which encouraged searching faith. And so they are often frightened or disturbed by adolescents who are struggling to enlarge their affiliative faith to include searching faith.'[8]

Stage Four: Owned Faith (adults)

Here the person has worked through the other existing stages of faith and now has their own. They are characterized by what they believe and readily look for ways to witness as a way of responding to their owned faith.

It's here that Westerhoff clearly suggests that confirmation should take place. Having worked through the other three stages, the person is now in a place of recognizing and owning their own faith and wanting to grow in it.

I worked with an amazing group of young people for about six years (yes, all young people are amazing, but these were especially amazing and I'm naturally completely biased). As we all grew in years and in faith during my time as a youth worker at their church, not deliberately structuring our youth work around Westerhoff's four stages of faith development, but nevertheless seeing links and connections with a number of his theories, we arrived at a place where they were driven by their faith to do something for those around them. We set up a community project including a social action weekend, concert and family fun day. It was brilliant, despite only a very select crowd at the concert, and there was a tangible vibration of the Spirit of God in that community. At the end of the weekend we had an evangelistic service, which the young people had organized, and I remember one interesting question in the midst of this amazing weekend when it came to the planning of the service. We had simply asked someone to do something in the service and the question came 'Can I do this even if I'm not confirmed?'. It should be stated at this point that we hadn't asked a thirteen-year-old to administer communion, marry or baptize anyone. My immediate reaction to the question was 'of course', but it created so many more questions for me.

Despite a move forward in communion before confirmation in many churches in recent years, the majority would indicate that communion can/should/ought to be taken after confirmation. But are we using confirmation as more of a hurdle to jump before we are 'allowed to do things in church', than a faith rite of passage? My response to this young person's question may well have been different and more exploratory if they had said 'I'm not sure I have enough faith to do what you are asking me to do.' The young person's need to ask the question as they did, makes me wonder if, with confirmation, we have drawn a line in the sand of what we think they should and shouldn't do in church and by that determined where they are in their faith journey without giving any credence to their own experience and understanding of God. Has confirmation become an unhelpful benchmark by which we determine what a young person can do and, more importantly, believe?

What I love about working with young people is that every day through their words, actions, reflections and behaviour, they remind me of their fabulous uniqueness and that they don't neatly fit any structure or developmental theory. They are out of the box and that's where they should stay – individual in their identity, their experience, their faith and their response to the gospel. To align them strictly to a tick-box attitude to faith development isn't really going to help anyone, but it might guide our reflections on confirmation and preparation by being driven to explore with our young people *their* faith in a less conventional way that we might have done before.

Chapter 5

Rites of Passage

Pete Maidment

American Pie

Just before writing this chapter, I had the opportunity to go and listen to the Australian sociologist and youth ministry specialist Fuzz Kitto, speaking at a training day at the London Institute for Contemporary Christianity. His subject was youth discipleship in a mission context and his aim was to help delegates explore what discipleship might look like in a secular/post-Christian society.

At the end of the talk, never wanting to miss a chance to research the future for confirmation, I asked whether Fuzz believed that confirmation still had a place in current youth culture. Fuzz's answer was succinct: 'Young people need good rites of passage: without good rites of passage being given to them they will invent rites of passage of their own. Just look at the movie *American Pie* if you want to see what kinds of rites of passage young people will invent left to their own devices.'[1]

The film *American Pie* tracks the lives of a group of high school students as they reach the end of their school year and prepare for the prom. For them this is the ultimate coming-of-age moment, when they can ditch school and move on to college or work. The young men in the film, in the absence of any more constructive rite of passage being offered them, devise their own, and so prom night, as well as being the night when the end of school is celebrated, becomes the night when they become men, by drinking and, primarily, by having sex for the first time.

Needless to say, things don't go so smoothly (this is Hollywood after all): some are unsuccessful in their quest, but discover a different level of maturity through that supposed failure; others are successful beyond their wildest dreams (the school dork's metamorphosis into a self-assured sexual diva is particularly memorable) while the lead character Jim (Jason Briggs) has the tables turned on his bullish chauvinistic intentions by his far-more-sexually-assured female counterpart, musician, Michelle (Alyson Hannigan).[2]

Whatever the outcomes, Hollywood's idea of what a contemporary teenage rite of passage should consist of is fairly obvious, and has at least a hint of accuracy. You can claim to be an adult when you've drunk a bit, smoked a bit and had sex . . . job done.

Jason Gardner hypothesizes that, for many young people, the rites of passage they invent are more about trying to look like adults than actually becoming adults. 'Attempting to look old enough to buy cigarettes is followed by trying to look old enough to get served in a pub, to buy alcohol at an off-licence, or to get into a nightclub. [Nineteen-year-old writer Sophie Hart-Walsh] concurs: "most of my adolescence has been spent trying to work out how not to seem like a teenager – how to appear much older and more mature. My friends and I learnt quickly. Wearing too much makeup and a pencil skirt on the bus in the hope that we would be charged full fare . . ."'[3]

This chapter explores the importance of good rites of passage for young people, looks at the effect that such rites have had in the past and, hopefully, demonstrates that, far from being an outdated concept, confirmation has lots to offer our young people in terms of a positive experience and positive step-off point into the world of the adult.

Puberty rites of passage

To avoid confusion: throughout this chapter we will refer to Puberty Rites Of Passage as PROPS – a clever acronym we're sure you'll agree. Later in the chapter we'll write about 'props' as a noun, which makes the acronym even cleverer but also makes the chapter a little bit difficult to navigate. So, when you read PROPS (capitalized) read Puberty Rites Of Passage and when you read props (lower case) read the noun to describe something that holds another thing up.

We are also conscious that we mostly refer to Puberty Rites of Passage (PROPS) with reference to young men. For this we apologize. While there appears to be an abundance\ of writing on PROPS for young men it is harder to find similar writing on the subject with reference to young women. Similarly, it's very easy to identify good study and writing on work with boys, but again more difficult to discover the same level of writing on work with girls. The obvious implication we might give is that it's only young men that need good rites of passage. That certainly isn't the case. We don't believe that young women are just passengers in this discussion or that the issues that affect them are in any way less important or less significant that the issues that affect young men.

In his book, *Boys Becoming Men,* Lowell Shepherd writes about the importance of providing Puberty Rites of Passage (PROPS). Writing specifically about young men, Shepherd notes that a breakdown in the father/son relationship and displacement from their extended families has had a devastating effect on boys. He talks about the struggle young men face with trying on their identities: boys naturally want to impress girls, but being 'macho' seems not to be 'in' any more, while simultaneously boys are uncomfortable with being 'feminine'. What is more, the whole of culture seems to be against the young man, with post-modernism itself offering the final stumbling block to the developing young man; it could easily be argued that boys thrived in the rigid and the rational of modernism, and are awash in the fluid of the post-modern world. Zygmunt Bauman writes that post-modernity is a 'license to do whatever one may fancy' and 'the exhilarating freedom to pursue anything and the mind-boggling uncertainty as to what is worth pursuing.'[4] For a young man arguably in need of structure and boundaries, this kind of world might be more than he can possibly cope with.

Pete's reflection

Perhaps my story might make this a little clearer. It seems
that in the past it was fairly clear what being a man meant.
You were the bread winner, the head of the household, it
was your responsibility to hunt and provide for your family
and they were to depend on you. The man was clearly top
of the ladder and his role was very clear. While today we
might struggle with that (and I'm not saying that it's
necessarily the correct view of what man should be), it is a
clear and straightforward goal for a young man to aim for
as he grows up. As I grew up I genuinely had no real sense
of what my role was. If I'm being honest, I felt (feel?) guilty
about who I am and what I represent. I am a white,
middle-class male. Pretty much everything that is wrong
with the world is my fault . . . As a young man growing up
in this culture, which lauds the underdog and the minority,
I was pretty much as unfashionable as I could get. This left
me with the feeling that I couldn't assert myself, I had lost
all rights to who I could be and what I could do. (I'm now
fighting the urge to apologize for what I've written, and
I'm picturing people reading this chapter, tutting and
huffing and muttering 'he doesn't know how lucky he is,
what is he complaining about?' . . . sorry . . . um . . . yes.)

The point is that I am sure that I am not the only one who feels this
way. Boys are lagging behind in school, and commit the vast majority
of crime. And yet at the same time men still earn more than women
and occupy more positions of authority. Basically we live in a society
where we guiltily occupy the seat at the head of the table, even
though we don't really want to, or deserve to. As a young man I simply
don't understand what my role is.

'Overwhelmed?' Shepherd asks at the end of this rather bleak picture.
Well, we needn't be, he continues.

The problem is that we often view adolescence as a negative thing: it's about just trying to get through. For some reason, society often views crisis as something to be avoided at all costs. The truth about crisis, particularly for the adolescent, is that it's what makes us grow. When the adolescent reaches a crisis and then with the help of friends, family and youth leaders, works through it, they grow. In his book, *Identity: Youth and Crisis*, the great psychologist Eric Homburger Erikson writes that it is crisis that marks our passage through childhood. As a person moves through childhood, Erikson argues, they come up against eight crisis stages. Each crisis, when resolved, marks an important moment in their journey towards achieving a healthy identity as an adult. When a young person doesn't face crises, and doesn't resolve those moments of identity formation, they are left less well prepared to face the challenges of adulthood.[5] Rather than something to be feared and avoided, crisis is a necessary (although uncomfortable) part of growing up.

For centuries in the West, children became adults through marked moments, distinct rites of passage; whether that was starting an apprenticeship or a job, or getting married. It's only really through the passage of the twentieth century that we've allowed generations to lurch from one stage to another rather than assisting in a smooth transition.[6]

In his book, *The Rites of Passage*, Arnold van Gennep, the man attributed with coining the phrase 'rite of passage' as we understand it today, explains that the initiation rite is performed in order to mark a separation from an old status, that of the child, and an incorporation into a new status, that of the adult, with the passing through of a middle stage he terms as 'liminality', where the initiate has no clear-cut status.[7]

Our picture of a native initiation rite is probably coloured by all sorts of different images and stories presented to us by the media, but there is no doubt that in many cultures the initiatory rite is something of a gruesome affair. Native Australians mark the passage to manhood of their boys with a ceremony involving circumcision and the pulling of a tooth. Native South Africans remove the tip of the little finger above the last joint. Other traditions involve cutting off the ear lobe, piercing the ear or the septum or scarring the initiate in some other way. The point of the native initiatory rite is to mark the initiate out as separate; 'the mutilated individual is removed from the common mass of humanity . . .'[8] (Interestingly, the rite of confirmation requires no external change to take place, presumably because it is assumed that the change that has happened within the initiate, of which confirmation is a symbol, should be visible enough without any external marking or mutilation.) By comparison, the risk of mild boredom or confusion that may be engendered by the traditional Anglican confirmation service seems like a very gentle way to mark your passage into adulthood.

Writing in *New Internationalist* magazine, Cameron Forbes observes the young aboriginal boy entering his initiatory ceremony. For this boy (aged between eleven and thirteen), it started seven days ago with his circumcision.

> Tonight, accompanied by an adult protector he will observe intricate dances and listen to complex songs from the *kirda* (owner) of the clan territory. The rite is full of mystery and wonder, some parts the boy can watch and others he has to turn his back on as they are still secret. At the end of the ceremony the boy will be sent out into the bush to help him connect with the Dreamtime; the 'Golden Age in Aborigine mythology, the heroic age when superbeings burst thorugh the earth's surface and performed monumental deeds'. It's a 'tradition which instructs both children and parents on how to cope with the crisis [of adolescence]'. Forbes notes, a stark contrast to what we in the west do, which is to 'Cross fingers and hope for the best'.[9]

In terms of symbolism, confirmation probably has far more in common with the bar mitzvah custom of the Judaic tradition. Bar mitzvah (literally 'a son of laws') marks the moment when a thirteen-year-old

Jewish boy, and more recently thirteen-year-old girl in the bat mitzvah ceremony, takes on the mantle of an adult worshipping Jew. However, in comparison to the six or so weeks of preparation that we might insist on for a young person coming to confirmation, the preparation for bar mitzvah is 'arduous'. The journey may take anything up to two or three years 'and includes Jewish history, religious ritual and classes in Hebrew, the ancient language of Judaism. The bar mitzvah candidate must become fluent enough to read and understand the basics of the language. And he must commit to memory the portion of the Torah (the Jewish holy book) that he is assigned to read on his bar mitzvah day.'[10] The writer continues by explaining that far from simply being learnt by rote to impress onlookers on the day, the learning involves deep discussion and discourse with friends and family. By the time the young man (or woman) comes to read the portion of the Scripture to the assembled crowds, he not only knows the passage off by heart but furthermore he understands it – deeply.

What a contrast that is to the few weeks I spent in the chaplain's office at school fudging my way through the 'Journey into Life' booklet.

One of the elements that stands out for me so powerfully about these experiences is the picture of community that they invoke. Writing about the aboriginal ritual, Forbes notes that the boy doesn't decide when he is ready to be initiated; in fact it's not even left to his father. Rather, all his relatives, by blood or by ritual, advise the boy and prepare him. The same with the bar mitzvah: it's assumed that the candidate will speak with family and friends as part of their preparation; the whole community seems to be involved.

Left to their own devices young people struggle to find ways to mark their passage to adulthood. If *American Pie* demonstrates the risks of allowing young people to devise their own rites of passage, then William Golding's *Lord of the Flies* paints an even bleaker picture. Left on an island (surely the perfect setting for an adolescent rite of passage) the boys quickly fall to pieces resorting to horrific bullying and power play. Terry Pratchett paints a much more idyllic picture in his novel *Nation*. In this book, Mau, the chief protagonist, travels to Boys' Island equipped with just his knife. He must survive on the Island for thirty days during which he must build the canoe which will carry him home. Mau has lain awake in the weeks running up to his separation from the tribe worrying about how he will build the canoe with just a knife; the fact that so many have done it before is the only thing that assures him it must be achievable.

> On his second day on the Boys' Island he found it.

> . . . Carved deeply into [the huge tabago tree's] dry bark in the language for children were the signs: MEN HELP OTHER MEN. Next to it, wedged into the wood, was an *alaki*, a carved black stone on a long handle. Hold it one way, it was an axe. Hold it the other, it was an adze, good for hollowing out a log.

> He pulled out the axe, and learned the lesson. So had many other boys. Mau climbed the tree one evening and found the hundreds of marks all the way up the trunk where generations of grateful boys had left the axe, or one like it, for those who came after.[11]

Native rites of passage remind us that young people need the presence and the company of adults, of those who have gone before. Maxine Green and Chandhu Christian in their book, *Accompanying*, write about the importance of young people being accompanied by adults as they journey.[12] The Church of England report *On the Way* uses the more traditional language of a sponsor; describing them as someone who 'shares his own faith journey and helps the candidate to articulate and thus evaluate and value his own'[13] and while it may seem more fashionable to suggest that young people can be left to get on by themselves, it's at our peril and their damage that we don't attempt to journey with them.

The Bible too has stories of young people who found maturity and adulthood through some kind of rite of passage: the boy David finds his feet on the day he slays Goliath on the battle field, Joseph journeys from arrogant daddy's boy to wise ruler of Egypt through a long and tortuous journey riddled with betrayal and suffering. We even get a wonderful insight into Jesus' maturation as he learns obedience after abandoning his parents in Jerusalem shortly after his twelfth birthday.

Props

While van Gennep finds the term 'Puberty Rite of Passage' unhelpful (explaining that rites of passage are rarely tied down to something even as variable as puberty), Shepherd keeps the term because of the strength of the word 'prop'. A PROP he explains can be well explained by the varied meanings of the word 'prop' . . . stick with this, it will make sense.

In the theatrical world a prop is a tool used by an actor to enhance a scene. It's a temporary artefact that would never be used for everyday purposes, but used in the right way by a skilled actor it adds depth and meaning to a scene. A rite of passage, Shepherd continues, should do much the same. It should be a magic moment which will live on in memory. The rite of passage should enable the child and the community to mark a point in time when one of life's corners was turned.

You may be thinking that confirmation does this, and certainly, compared to many of our church services, confirmation does carry a sense of drama, if nothing else because of the presence of the bishop in all his regalia. But, compared to the drama and excitement that accompanies the rites of passage for other religions and traditions, confirmation may feel a little like the poor cousin.

Author Michele Guinness writes about her huge disappointment with Christian rites of passage. Forced to leave the Jewish family she grew up in when she became a Christian, Michelle was saddened by the lack of occasion at her baptism – 'no wrestling my way to the buffet table (there was no food at all), no being spun like a top in the centre of a circle of dancing viragos (dancing was a taboo in the church in those days), no presents (too unspiritual) and little to suggest the entrance to membership of a community'. Of confirmation she continues '[it's not] a "coming-of-age" in its truest sense. Candidates play a very small part in the service, which often has no immediate or obvious practical consequence or access to what are regarded as strictly "adult" roles – leading prayers, reading lessons, or becoming a member of the church council. The service is rarely followed by any kind of festivities.'[14]

When used as a verb, Shepherd continues, a prop is a support (as in 'to prop up'). I'm currently sitting looking out into my garden and I can see broad beans growing up the canes that I have given them for support. Each time the beans grow another few inches I am careful to tie them on to the poles. Apparently it's not entirely necessary, but my garden is a bit exposed and so the poles or props I've provided give the young plants support against the wind as they grow to maturity. The props don't stop the wind, they don't reduce the turbulence, they simply provide the support that my young plants need in order to withstand the buffeting of the elements. Confirmation then should act a little like those canes in my garden, it should help our young people find the prop that they need in order to wade through the tumult of adolescence; a young person should be able to look back to their confirmation and remember that it was at that moment that the Church acknowledged them to be an adult; recognized the God-given gifts that he or she has and responded appropriately. Confirmation should be a very real tie into a community that will care for one of its own and lend adult support and guidance. It should also be the act that the young person can refer to when the Church is not forthcoming with responding to the young person as an adult. When the young person feels that their faith or their journey isn't taken seriously, they should be able to respond by saying, 'But you confirmed me, you acknowledged my maturity, that means I need to be taken seriously as an adult.' Adolescence really is one of the toughest parts of life. Jason Gardner, in his book *Mend the Gap*, quotes Hazel a sixteen-year-old who describes adolescence as being 'like a tightrope walk from the secure, safe platform of childhood to adulthood. Suddenly the world becomes a difficult and dangerous balancing act – which the whole world seems to be watching.'[15] It's notable that Hazel refers to adolescence as being like a tightrope, a concept already unpacked in Chapter 3. The Church needs to celebrate the fact that it can offer such a great support for our young people as they make that journey.

Finally, Shepherd explains that to a sailor a prop is the part of a boat or ship that propels it forward. Used well a Puberty Rite Of Passage can act as the impetus that a young person needs to drive them on into the next part of life, to give them the push that they need to step out and take on the role of an adult in the Church and beyond.

Fertile ground

Anne Richards, editor of the Church of England's landmark book *Through the Eyes of a Child*, talks about one young person's response to the offer of confirmation. This teenager, she explains, wrote about confirmation that it was offered as a rubicon to be crossed, an invitation to 'leave the world of childhood behind and join us adults on the other side'. He didn't much fancy it, finding more fellowship and discipleship with his friends on social networking sites than with the adult company of Christians he was being offered.[16]. The young man Anne refers to is called Philip and this is what he writes:

> I got told off for asking questions and 'mucking about', but I felt that with all my friends in the confirmation group we were really getting somewhere. When we went on retreat we stayed up talking and having fun and when we talked about heaven and hell I found that others my age have the same thoughts and dreams as me. It was great. Lots of friends from the confirmation group are on MSN and we're always texting and emailing each other, and so many of the things we share come from our thoughts about the Christian faith. But it's cool, not like sitting in rows and being talked at.[17]

I find this deeply saddening. When the young person looked at the adult Church into which he was meant to be confirmed, he wasn't interested, preferring instead the fellowship offered by people of his own age. Fuzz Kitto, at the training morning mentioned earlier, spoke of the importance of fertile ground if we want our young people to grow up well discipled in the Church. If a young person comes down from their group to church and sees a congregation that doesn't model what true discipleship should look like, the likelihood is that they will leave disappointed.

The irony is that for generations young people have usually been ahead of the adult church in trying to find new ways of being church, of modelling what true discipleship might look like.

Philip's chapter in *Through the Eyes of a Child* is provocative and deeply challenging. It's an incredible insight into the world of a teenage boy and his wrestling with his faith. It also sums up some of the real tensions that young people feel as church members. Philip says that much of his Christian teaching has consisted of being told to sit down and listen rather than giving a sense of *journeying* with adults. And so his conclusions are drawn from a mixture of what he has been told in church, what he has seen and read in films and books and what he has chatted about with his friends.

We believe that young people need the chance to sit down with adults and to bounce ideas and reflections off them. To wrestle through doubts and questions, rather than simply be told the answers. Young people need to know that adults have doubts and questions and they need to be able to explore those with them. In a recent article for *Immerse*, an American youth ministry journal, the youth ministry expert Andrew Root writes that 'Christianity is about living in opposition to certainty; it is about faith in the midst of doubt'. 'A good confirmation teacher', he continues, 'is not someone who knows every answer. It is someone who can create an environment where people feel safe enough to speak their deepest doubts into the life of the group, to speak those doubts and then seek God in them. The job of the confirmation leader is to invite doubts to be spilled without fear of shock or dehumanizing judgment from others'.[18] When a young person grows up in the church with little or no desire to be like the adults she sees in the pews around her, it seems likely that she has had little chance to explore the faith with them in the way Professor Root describes.

Let me offer my church as an example. I am privileged to be involved in leading our eleven- to fourteen-year-old group of Pathfinders on a Sunday morning. It's a small group sometimes attracting just a couple of young people and sometimes drawing seven or eight members. Each week we head upstairs after the first few songs in church for our own time together. We have decided to keep our morning meetings as simple as possible, so we provide breakfast for the group (second breakfast for some of them) of croissants and hot chocolate, and then we ask them how their week has been. That's pretty much it. We usually finish with a thought or a reflection and something for them to take into the week with them, usually around the topic of looking for God in all things, but that's as complex as our meetings get.

We have realized that the young people really crave time to chat and to have an adult who will simply listen to them. They don't want to be 'taught' anything. We view discipleship as the process of accompanying young people and helping them to look for God in their ordinary lives.

At the same time, we are also trying to rethink how we do our main service on a Sunday morning, the service that the young people currently escape from. Can you guess some of the elements that people are suggesting for our new-look 11.15 meeting? You've got it, food, fellowship, freedom to choose activities and space to spend time and grow together.

Without those changes I fear for the young people who will shortly be leaving Pathfinders to head back into the 'church' proper. They will go from a model of church that is about being together and sharing life, to a model of church that is (largely) focused on the front and individualistic.

'Fresh expressions' and 'Mission-shaped' are terms that we have become very familiar with in the Church of England over the last few years. For the most part we are coming to our senses in terms of recognizing that if we are to be a church 'fit for purpose' then we need to re-evaluate and rethink our worship and our communities. In the book *Mission-shaped Youth*, Tim Sudworth brings together stories of how churches across the UK have successfully rethought their approach to what it means to be church in order to create spaces where young people can be effectively discipled and encouraged. He quotes Archbishop Rowan Williams's memorable phrase calling for a more 'mixed economy' – 'recognizing church where it appears and having the willingness and skill to work with it'.[19] A call to think in fresh ways about how we do church for young people, must surely include a call to rethink how we approach the rites of passage that we offer.

The rite of passage that we have in confirmation contains all of the necessary ingredients for the young person to make that step off into the world of the adult. The commission that the bishop speaks over the initiate is both daunting and challenging, leaving little room for doubt that this young person is taking on a full adult faith and full adult responsibilities. During this commission the young person will promise, with the help of God, to

> continue in the Apostles' teaching and fellowship,
> in the breaking of bread, and in prayers . . .
> persevere in resisting evil,
> and, whenever you fall into sin, repent and return
>   to the Lord . . .
> proclaim by word and example
> the good news of God in Christ . . .
> seek and serve Christ in all people,
> loving your neighbour as yourself . . .
> acknowledge Christ's authority over
>   human society,
> by prayer for the world and its leaders,
> by defending the weak, and by seeking peace and justice.[20]

This stuff is rocket fuel! They are amazing promises, and awe-inspiring too if we take them seriously. But even more important is that they are the final promises we'll be expected to make. It's not like these are promises we make as young people, followed by further more serious promises as an adult. No! This is it. These are the promises and this is the rite that will mark our moving on into adult faith!

There is nothing to stop us from making the confirmation experience as grand and exciting and as joyful as we want it to be; the dream being that the young person finishes the service and for the rest of their life looks back on the day as a moment of huge significance for them, both in the development of their faith as well as their growth.

This is all very well, but it does mean that we have to take seriously the rite of passage that we have been given. We need to learn from other rites of passage and discover what we can add to ours to get the best out of it. This means several things.

First, it means taking the confirmed young person seriously as an adult. In other cultures the initiate is no longer viewed as a child, instead they take on the full roles and responsibilities of an adult worshipper or member of the community.

Second, it means giving the young people we bring to confirmation all the support that we can give them. Praying for them, giving them adults who they can spend time with, who will listen to them and lead them.

It means doing the best we can in our preparation. Providing the best input and support we can offer that will help the young people view their faith as something that can really make a difference in their lives.

Finally, it means viewing the celebration as a stepping point, rather than an end point. While the confirmation service remains the end of the journey, we are failing our young people. It would be far better to view the ceremony as a mid-point in their discipleship.

There is no doubt that we live in a culture that is desperate for good, healthy rites of passage for our adolescents. The question remains, can we reinvigorate confirmation in such a way that it becomes that rite?

Chapter 6

The Passing Out Parade

Pete Maidment with Tim Sledge

Three vicars are chatting at the end of a meeting. The first says that he has had terrible trouble with bats in his building, and that he's desperate to get rid of them. Knowing that it's against the law to disturb bats, the other two lean in closer so as not to be overheard.

'We tried ringing the bells for twenty-four hours to celebrate our patronal festival,' continues the first vicar, 'and after ten hours the bats got so sick of the noise that every last one of them flew away. Trouble was no sooner had the last note died than they all flew straight back in.'

'We tried something similar,' adds the second, 'we held a twenty-four-hour alternative worship prayer event, and we burnt incense throughout the whole period, right under the bell tower. After ten hours,' he goes on, 'every bat flew out of the belfry, they couldn't stand all that smoke. Trouble is, when we eventually extinguished the incense, no sooner had the last wisp of smoke drifted out of the door than *whoosh* every single bat shot straight back in.'

The third vicar looks left and right to make sure that no one is listening and then leans in even closer. 'We've cracked it,' she whispers. Looking impressed, the other two lean in closer still, 'we confirmed the lot of them and we haven't seen them since!'

There's a lot of anecdotal evidence around which maintains that confirmation has come to represent little more than a passing out parade for young people. It's one of those statistics that is difficult to pin down because, of course, the young people you want to count are no longer there. The Church of England is good at keeping track of who is being confirmed, but less well adept at following what happens to them after the service has finished.

Throughout this and subsequent chapters we will start to refer to some of the research that we undertook in preparation for writing this book. We worked with Diocesan Youth Officers (DYOs) across the UK to find people's views and experiences of the confirmation process, with two separate pieces of research. We composed a survey, which we rolled out twice with two different methods. First, members of a small working group of DYOs interested in working together on confirmation visited groups across their respective dioceses. We met with small groups of young people and talked through the questions in the survey. This was a really helpful process as it enabled us to listen to what young people were saying and to discuss with them what they felt. These groups spanned churches from across the nation and of differing traditions, but we felt that it was also important to try to get the broadest feedback possible. So we rewrote the original questions and set them up as an online survey, again calling on the national network of DYOs for their support in finding answers to our questions. The research was for people up to fifty years of age who had been confirmed between the ages of eight and twenty-five.[1] Of the 242 people who responded to the online questionnaire, 129 people provided complete responses. Of those, 64 per cent were female and 36 per cent were male. 54 per cent of our respondents lived in a suburban setting, 30 per cent rural and 17 per cent lived in an urban setting. While we won't be so bold as to use this research to make any sweeping statements about young people's attitudes towards confirmation, it does give some interesting figures for us to consider, and a wonderful array of thoughts and reflections.

In talking with Pete before starting this book, Paul Butler, Bishop of Southwell and Nottingham, referred to his own experience of being confirmed as a teenager and returning to church to discover that no one else from his preparation group had continued to attend and how he himself stopped shortly after. *Youth Apart*, the Church of England's vision document for young people from 1996 acknowledges that 'some people have said that many see confirmation as a "rite of passage" out of the church rather than as a ceremony of welcome into the worshipping community'.[2] And sitting down with Tim Sledge (Vicar of Romsey Abbey and co-author of the *Youth Emmaus* course, among other titles) in order to write this chapter, we'd barely finished our first chip (we were in a pub) before he had referred to confirmation with the words, 'the passing out parade'.

It seems that whatever the statistical evidence, and we know only too well the rate at which teenagers have been leaving our churches, the perception is that young people come to confirmation and the cake crumbs from the after-service bunfight have barely been swept away before they've left the church.

Why is this? What is it about our system of preparation and follow up that means our young people find it so hard to remain in the church after they're confirmed? This was my question when I sat down with Tim to pull this chapter together. In a previous conversation I had mentioned that I was halfway through this project and wondered what his thoughts were on confirmation. His answer straight away was that he felt the way we prepare young people for the rite was all wrong.

What follows is some of our conversation one day in Romsey with thoughts and reflections along the way.

I started off by asking Tim what he felt the purpose of confirmation was.

Tim: I think I've always struggled with what the purpose of confirmation is because it just feels like a passing out parade really. I think it's the first time you liturgically call the Holy Spirit down on somebody, intentionally. For what purpose? I believe in confirmation, it is the power to live the apostolic life. It's the 'unction to function', the energy or the capacity to function at an age, whatever age that is, to be able to live that life.

Pete: What has the Holy Spirit been doing up to that point, in that person's life?

Tim: The Holy Spirit's been active in that person's life from the point
of baptism. If baptism is a sacrament (I don't think anybody's
going to argue with that one), and a sacrament, to quote
Richard Giles, is 'when God shows up'. In other words, in the
sacraments, there's a dead sure thing that whatever we do,
God shows up. If baptism is about integration into the life of
the Church and the light of Christ shining in that person, then
the gift bestowed at confirmation is to say, 'You've had that
light shining in you, now release that light. Go and share it
with other people. Go and live a Christ-like, apostolic life.'
Confirmation is so tied in with Pentecost and that's the change
that happened with the disciples. We *could* argue that
Pentecost was the disciple's confirmation.

This interested me because you will remember that in an earlier
chapter we talked about how many people find it important for a
person of apostolic succession to lay hands on the candidate in order
to impart the transforming grace of the Holy Spirit. My suspicion is that
this serves as another example of the Church's habit of sacralizing its
actions. It's like we've got so caught up with the hands, and whose
hands and so on that we miss what happens. It's the moment when
the Holy Spirit is intentionally invoked in someone's life, and while the
presence of the bishop certainly adds the drama previously referred to,
it's not his *hands* that are important, but rather the work of the Holy
Spirit that changes the person.

A further interesting reflection occurred as I read through the responses
to the research we had done. Of the 142 people who answered the
question 'Why did you get confirmed?', only one person mentioned
the work of the Holy Spirit: 'I . . . was looking for the Holy Spirit.' Of
those who answered the question 'What does confirmation mean to
you?', there were three more mentions of the Spirit: 'an
acknowledgement of the importance of the Holy Spirit for our lives', 'to
. . . receive the Holy Spirit as strength and guide for the journey' and
'laying on of hands, as the apostles did and praying for the
strengthening of God's Holy Spirit'.

Having ascertained very briefly what Tim's thoughts were on the overall meaning and purpose of confirmation I was keen to explore further what his thoughts were on how we prepare the young for the rite and whether this had any impact on young people or the Church viewing the rite as a passing out parade. I started by asking Tim to talk me through a picture of how the Church, generally speaking, approaches confirmation with young people.

The hothouse effect

Tim: At the moment, the norm is that (for the only time in their Christian lives almost) we *hothouse* young people. We ram a whole load of doctrine down their throats so that they can answer all of the questions in the confirmation service without having to cross their fingers behind their backs. Now I know that's slightly a parody of a general approach, but at the end of that hothousing we confirm them and then we provide no further place of nurture and growth.

And we expect our young people to survive.

No wonder if you go through your confirmation registers, 80 per cent of your confirmands haven't stayed, because they've died; they've withered on the vine. It seems to me that when you leave a greenhouse you have three options: one is you die; we plant you out with everyone else . . .

Pete: . . . in the cold and damp . . .

Tim: . . . and you die. Another is that after you have been planted out, you adapt to your surroundings and you do grow. The third option is that you think the greenhouse is so lovely you want to build another one and you think that the whole world is like confirmation classes. Fifty or sixty years ago that was fine, because when you planted out a confirmation candidate they could actually survive. But spiritually our culture has done the opposite of global warming, we've had a little bit of global 'spiritual chilling', the world is much cooler to Christian values and it is so hard – especially as a young person – to survive in these conditions.

I imagine that any of us who have worked with young people will have experienced the effects of this kind of spiritual hothousing. As a youth worker I used to take my youth group to Soul Survivor. At the beginning of the event I remember that we pretty much had to impose a health warning to cover the next five days. We had to explain that while Soul Survivor was going to be an amazing experience and that in all likelihood they would all meet with God and grow, at the end of the week we would have to return to real life. That church as we know it would have stayed the same, the music would be less impressive, the sermons less engaging and less entertaining. Soul Survivor was definitely the hothouse, and the young people needed to be prepared for the bump at the end of the week. I can remember several young people and one in particular who had incredible experiences at the festival and met with God in a profound way, but once they returned to real life it all drifted away. The hothouse is great for a quick burst of growth, but anyone who has started their seedlings off under the protection of glass and then taken them outside before the last frost, will know the devastating effect a night out in the real world can have on growth and health.

Tim: Put it this way: imagine that I'm a young person. For eight or ten weeks you've put me in a greenhouse and you feed me with a load of stuff and all of a sudden you take an interest in me. Every week or every fortnight you meet and you're talking about the Bible and God in a way that you might not with any other people.

Our survey asked people who it was that prepared them for their confirmation. 72 per cent of the respondents said it was an ordained person. This reflects our experience as youth workers; we found that more often than not the vicar wanted to run the confirmation preparation. And for good reason: they see that confirmation is important and so they want to be involved with the process. Problems may arise if the vicar (or curate) isn't the person who usually interacts with the young people and therefore isn't intimately involved with that young person's discipleship. The danger in these cases is that the young people either return to their original group without the person who accompanied them through the confirmation preparation, or in many cases they simply have nothing to go to. The group has finished and so has their discipleship.

Pete's experience

At the church where I worked we had a kind of compromise, the vicar wanted to be involved with the preparation and so he and I led the group together. Which was fine. It meant that I was with the young people as they went through their preparation and I would continue to meet with them after the confirmation service. The problem, in hindsight, was that because the vicar only attended the confirmation preparation, it kind of implied that this part of the young person's discipleship was somehow more important than any other part. It gave the confirmation preparation a kind of 'otherly' feel, and while it's important that confirmation be taken seriously, it seems a great shame if that then makes the rest of the discipleship journey for the young person feel kind of second place.

The problem with this hothouse style of preparation is that it leaves the young person feeling that by being confirmed they have simply ticked a box on a list – and that the Church is doing the same. Tim clarified this point with a story about an experience he had had in Romsey.

Tim: We had an example locally of a mum who rang up and said 'My son got confirmed two years ago and he didn't get a Bible.' And I said 'Well who is your son? I don't know who he is. Does he come to anything we do?' 'No.' 'Is he an active worshipper somewhere? How's he doing in his Christian faith?' I was trying to be as nice as I could. For her, confirmation was a badge you get.

It's an interesting picture isn't it. When two years after the event a mum phones up because she's heard that at other churches young people get a gift and she feels that her son has missed out, you have to wonder what the motivation for getting confirmed was in the first place. Our research confirmed that there is a small but significant percentage of young people who get confirmed simply because it is the expected thing to do: of the 142 people who answered the question 'Why did you get confirmed?', twenty said that it was just something that people did at their church or that it was expected of them. Of those twenty, two said that it was something they felt compelled or forced to do. In fact nine out of the 142 said that being confirmed wasn't their choice.

For some it's as if confirmation is a GCSE: you work hard to learn all that you need to get through the exam and then once it's finished you get the certificate and move on to something different. It's another thing achieved, and it does not make much difference to the rest of life (as my inability to have even the simplest conversation in French attests, despite getting a B grade all those years ago).

So if preparing young people for confirmation using a course with a defined start and end point is unhelpful, what is the alternative? Tim was keen to work through a case study of what confirmation preparation could look like.

Tim: We've got so conditioned into running confirmation courses we think that confirmation is a sort of theology exam or we check that we can get the right answers. We need a shift of understanding of recognizing that confirmation preparation and the confirmation service are a pastoral rite as much as a missional and theological rite. It might be a part of our initiation, but it's all about how we care for and nurture our young people. Of course, they need to *learn* something, but actually I think we need a much higher understanding and doctrine of how we're going to care for them.

Soul buddies

Tim: In the confirmation service there's a critical bit which is missed by too many people and that's the offer of a soul friend or journey guide. You wouldn't baptize anyone without a godparent so I think you shouldn't confirm anyone without a journey guide.

When we were piloting the *Youth Emmaus* material with a church in Yorkshire they had a group that used it (as most of them do) for a confirmation course. There is a bit in there about having soul friends and all of the young people on the course had them. I went along to their penultimate meeting, assuming that the nine young people would all have got their parents or someone to be their soul friend. Everyone of them had an old aged pensioner as a buddy. They'd all chosen independently and it really was a massive thing for me. They saw them [their 'buddies'] as pillars of the faith and some of the older people then came on some of the course with them. In other words, if you're ninety you are journeying just as much as if you're thirteen. And that model, that principle is a really really good one. I'd love to see it happen in many more places.

Pete's experience

In scuba diving the concept of a buddy is well recognized. For safety reasons, most divers would say that you should never dive alone, but rather always enter the water with someone; a dive buddy. A dive buddy is there primarily for safety reasons: to assist in the case of an emergency such as a shortage of oxygen or an injury. For a new or inexperienced diver, the buddy also provides a reassuring presence and the experience that can prevent or avoid possible problems. A buddy also increases the enjoyment of a dive; by diving with someone you can share stories of what you saw beneath the waves. Like most of life's great experiences, the chance of sharing what you have done

> with another person only makes that experience more
> wonderful and more memorable.
>
> I've only been diving once, it was on my honeymoon and I
> discovered that I was a rubbish buddy! I was so blown
> away with the idea of being underwater that I completely
> forgot about my buddy (my wife of one week) and left her
> floundering on the surface while I splashed and swam with
> all the fishes.

It's not just the *Youth Emmaus* course that encourages young people to
adopt a buddy, the Anglican report *On The Way* encouraged a return to
the catechumenate model for young people approaching confirmation,
one element of which was the suggestion that they have a sponsor:

> An essential part of the Faith Journey as envisaged in the
> catechumenate is that it should be an accompanied one. The
> role of 'sponsor' is therefore highly significant. Essentially it is an
> Emmaus Road experience. The candidate and the sponsor walk
> together. The sponsor – a lay person – cares for and prays for
> the candidate and introduces the candidate to the rites. The
> sponsor shares his [or her] own faith journey and helps the
> candidate to articulate and thus evaluate his [or her] own.[3]

More recently, Mark Yaconelli's book, *Contemplative Youth Ministry*,
outlines a complete model of youth ministry based on youth leaders
accompanying young people on their spiritual journeys. In one section
he describes the role of the youth minister and in so doing draws a
wonderful picture of what a soul buddy might look like. Youth ministry
can be seen in four activities, writes Yaconelli: youth ministers *point*; like
John the Baptist, keeping our eyes and ears open to the presence of
God and seeking to help young people notice God. We should
question; constantly ready to ask young people 'How is God present?'
helping young people to acknowledge God in all things; Tim Sledge
speaks of this as recognizing that the world is a sacrament; having the
confidence to say that it's okay to be a Christian and that God is an

integral part of your daily life. The youth minister, Yaconelli continues, should *invite* young people to turn and notice God directly within their experience, we should invite them to pray in different ways and invite them to listen to and receive from God. Finally, the minister should *create circumstances*, 'it's circumstances, not ideas, that change people' says Yaconelli quoting Richard Rohr.[4] Possibly the most significant way we can help young people notice their experience of God is by helping them engage with real life. If we can help young people realize that their lives have already begun, that they're not waiting for university or adulthood or a job or marriage for *real* life to begin, but instead to see how God is already calling them to be a source of life and healing in this world, then we have done an incredible thing in making the apostolic life that they are being confirmed into a reality rather than just an exam in God theory.[5]

Having a soul buddy means having someone who journeys with you way beyond confirmation. It's someone with whom you can talk, pray and ask questions. It's also someone who can mark with you all of the incidental rites along the way. Confirmation might be the most noticeable or most public moment at which you affirm your faith but there are many other milestones along the way and having a soul buddy means having someone who will celebrate those moments with you. Whether it's the first time you lead prayers in church, or when you first lead a Bible study for your youth group or speak at a CU meeting. All those moments are important in the ongoing discipleship of a young person and are made even more powerful by the presence of a fellow traveler praying for you and celebrating with you.

Ditching the course?

As diocesan youth officers we're asked on a weekly basis if there are any good resources for young people and whether we can recommend any confirmation preparation courses. More often than not our answer is 'no'. It's not that there is nothing good in print, far from it, there are loads of really useful programmes and sessions out there (there are some suggestions in the Appendix). It's just that on their own they rarely fit the bill. It should come as no surprise really. Your group is quite unlike any other group in the world!

I wanted to know what Tim might suggest as an alternative to a confirmation course.

Tim: I am not opposed to a course, I just think that we take them off the shelf too quickly and fail to really think what questions young people actually have. I would start with the big questions: for example, if there are three questions you could ask God what would they be? I'd work on those to start with. Then you can use the courses available as a sort of buffet – pick and choose appropriate sessions. Once you've asked the young people what their three questions are you then might need to know that you can find help with answering those questions in this or that particular book. Increasingly people need to start picking out a bit of this and a bit of that and doing their own. All the stats on nurture, for all ages, say that the best course, by far and away is the home-grown one. So Alpha is used by say 25 per cent, Emmaus is used by 15 per cent but of those who have them I think it's 40 per cent go for a hybrid model. I also think that you are far more likely to keep young people this way as they will feel engaged and listened to from day one.

Pete's experience

This model of running a discipleship group has started successfully at the church where I am a volunteer youth worker. When I arrived we were using a published programme, which, although it had some good content, was clearly not designed for our group. For a start, we rarely had time to fit all of the material in and secondly we discovered that the material was often written assuming that the group were really 'on fire' in their faith. Our group meets for a short time (some times as little as twenty minutes) and for most of them, coming to church is just something that they do, they are exploring faith, but not necessarily ready to change the world just yet. The way we run the group now is that we meet for breakfast on a Sunday morning, and we talk about how the week has been. Each week we have just one reflection or one Bible story rather than trying to get all the way through a pre-planned weekly session. The thought of ditching the material was quite daunting. We felt that we would struggle to know what to do each week. Now, however, we feel relieved. Trying to fulfil the needs of the course material was far more stressful than simply meeting with the young people and working with them where they are. Sometimes we use an activity from the published course, sometimes we watch a video clip from YouTube that has a particular message or a clip from a DVD. Sometimes we'll just have a time of quiet or reflection. Whatever we do it's great to know that rather than just one book dictating our time we have a whole range of books and other sources to choose from. There is a selection of resources in the Appendix.

Back to the conversation with Tim.

The apostolic life

Pete: So it seems that the main role of confirmation is to prepare young people to live the apostolic life, to know what it means to live as a Christian.

Tim: With my young people I sometimes took them to a shopping arcade with an escalator and I would get them at the bottom of the one that was going down and I'd tell them to imagine trying to get to the top of it. We'd have a bit of a laugh thinking about what a disaster it would be, and I would say, 'The issue is, how are we going to walk up the escalator of life?' Because all of the values of life are coming down at you. We can make it, and the fun was that people would fall off and people would get in the way. But the lesson was that the values of the world are against us. And of course if any of them get to the top then they're exhausted! Because it is an exhausting thing to do. I don't think that the Church has realized just how hard it is to live the Christian life outside of the youth group or confirmation preparation course, and so therefore it's about saying we *know* it's hard and we want to help you and support you in doing that. When the disciples have received the power of the Holy Spirit in Acts it's not the end of the story, they then go back to meeting and devoting themselves to one another. Their apostolic life meant always going back to those things.

Pete: So confirmation preparation is about engaging young people with the real world and the reality of what it means to be a Christian? It's about spiritual disciplines? What else do you put in?

Tim: Some help with prayer, but most of it would be about Christian lifestyle: how we deal with other people; how we are in relationship with other people; how we live in the world; and how the Bible relates to the world today.

Final thoughts

In fact the confirmation service tells us exactly what young people need in order to continue in their faith and their spiritual growth after the service. Those five questions of the commission are a neat summing up of the apostolic life. And perhaps where we've failed is in helping young people to know how to live out that commission. We might have done a great job teaching them the right answers, but unless we are actually helping them to live that commissioning out then we are failing to make confirmation something that radically changes lives.

Let's just reflect again on the promises that the young people make in that all important commission after they have been confirmed:

> Will you continue in the apostles' teaching and fellowship,
> in the breaking of bread and in the prayers?

> Will you persevere in resisting evil,
> and whenever you fall into sin, repent and return to the Lord?

> Will you proclaim by word and example
> the good news of God in Christ?

> Will you seek and serve Christ in all people,
> loving your neighbour as yourself?

> Will you acknowledge Christ's authority over human society,
> by prayer for the world and its leaders,
> by defending the weak, and by seeking peace and injustice?[6]

To each of these questions the young person is expected to answer 'With the help of God, I will.'

Breathtaking isn't it? Go on, read them again!

We'll talk about what it means to treat a confirmed young person as an adult in a later chapter and we'll come back to that commission for a more in-depth study then. But for now it is enough to acknowledge that there is no way on earth that a few weeks of hothousing could ever prepare a young person to live out those promises; most of us adults who've been walking in faith for decades would struggle to say those promises now without a twinge of guilt. The only way to be able to live out that kind of commission is to be in a good, healthy discipleship process and that takes time, in fact it takes all the time we have.

I'll leave Tim's voice to be the last in this chapter. I asked him whether it was curtains for confirmation, whether it was the end for this rite of passage. He answered by considering where we've come with confirmation and what the future may hold.

Tim: The weakness of the old way of looking at confirmation was 'well now you're confirmed you can join in with us'. In other words, we've confirmed you and we've also conformed you. Does confirmation confirm something that was said for you at baptism? Does it conform you to the system of the Church? Or does it affirm you in the life that you choose to live now? If it's just saying yes to the first two, then don't do it! Too much of confirmation is conformation 'this is how the church runs and this is what you need to know about to find your place in church as it is now', which is just an imperialistic tool.

The way we did confirmation before meant that there was no need to live the Christian life, you just got confirmed, whereas now I find it quite hard to confirm someone who didn't at least have a vague idea of how all this was going to work. I think those five statements in the commission mean that our liturgy is catching up with our theology.

Chapter 7

What Does It Mean to Treat a Young Person as an Adult Christian?

How does confirmation affect the way that we treat young people in church? Do we view our children and young people in a new way once they have made these very adult promises, or once the service has finished do they return to the same status as before? As adults do we take seriously the words they have said in front of the bishop and their families and friends or, by our indifference, do we make those words meaningless?

These are tough questions, but if we want confirmation to make a difference, to really *mean* something, then we really do have to make certain that we recognize the change that has happened in a young person after the rite.

Pete's experience

When young people are allowed to take roles of responsibility in church it makes a difference. I can recall the first time that Alex, a young man who attended our Sunday evening group, was given permission to preach in an evening service. He was a strong Christian who I think we all suspected was destined for employed ministry of some kind and so he was an obvious choice for a young person to speak at church. His sermon was on the Holy Spirit, and, I'll be honest, it had lots of holes and flaws. He kept referring to the Holy Spirit as 'it' rather than 'he' and mostly he read his words rather than speaking from the heart. But those things didn't matter because he spoke honestly and with integrity. After the service one adult told me that it was the best sermon they had ever heard in the church, not in a patronizing 'let's applaud the youngster' kind of way, rather something about hearing such a young man of God (he was about sixteen at the time) had a profound effect on the listener. It was the same when Robert and Matt joined the PCC as teenagers, or Hannah took on leadership of the Pathfinder (eleven to fourteen) group or when Erica, Jeffrey and Tanya got involved in holiday club. Something about their youthfulness and their willingness to serve and lead and be involved was deeply captivating.

The Bible is full of examples of God using young people to do wonderful things. Joseph showed courage and strength in the face of unbelievable adversity, pursuing purity and holiness in the face of great temptation and showing wisdom, foresight and leadership. David, the young man left at home to tend the flocks while his grown up brothers went off to war, stood up to the greatest warrior that the Philistines had ever had. Gideon, when confronted by the angel of the Lord, declared his clan to be the 'weakest in Manasseh' and himself to be the 'least' in his family, a response that I've always thought to mean youngest (indeed for many years British Youth for Christ named their year out scheme 'Operation Gideon' in honour of this young man), and yet God used him to stand up and lead the nation of Israel as they fought to be free from the clutches of the Midianites. And of course we mustn't forget that Mary, Jesus' mother, was just a young teenager when she accepted God's call to carry and give birth to the Messiah. There is even much speculation that Jesus' disciples were mostly young men, making Jesus a first-rate youth worker. Jesus himself, as a young person, sat in the Temple courts and taught the oldest and the wisest of the teachers of the law (much to the horror of his parents as they searched the city for their missing son).

At other times we learn incredible things about faith from young people in the Bible. Isaac is surprisingly silent and unbelievably trusting when his father holds a knife to his throat. To think that this young man, and he is certainly no infant by this point, is so trusting of his father and his father's God is humbling beyond belief.

These young people all had things in common – for a start they all loved God. They were willing to take huge risks and to make huge sacrifices because they knew and loved their Heavenly Father. Joseph's love for God was so huge that even when faced with the temptation of sleeping with his boss's wife he ran away – for him purity was more important than pleasure. Gideon was happy to do something that as adults we struggle with – he questioned God; when the angel confronted him with the challenge to lead the Israelites he questioned, he wanted assurances and proof. I can remember as a young person feeling that I was taught that having questions or wanting proof meant I didn't have enough faith.

Jesus had an incredible heart for children too. When the disciples tried to chase the mothers and their babies away Jesus stepped in, took the children in his arms, and blessed them – a sure sign of his compassion and heart for the young, and when thousands of people were starving on a hillside Jesus took a small boy's gift of fish and bread and with it performed a great and wonderful miracle. I love the language that youth specialist Chap Clarke uses in the book *Starting Right* when he describes God's heart as 'decisively compassionate toward children'.[1]

God takes the young seriously!

Yet in the church it often feels as if the examples Pete gives at the start of this chapter are the exception rather than the rule. In their book, *Youth Work after Christendom*, Jo and Nigel Pimlott write about the culture of negativity that has grown up around young people. 'The myth that young people are the root of all evil is sadly popular', they write, '. . . at almost every opportunity, young people are demonized by the media and politicians, while members of local communities are quick to blame them for many of society's ills'.[2]

A recent study showed that more than four in five young people feel they are represented by the media as a group to be feared.[3] It's as if we have been taught culturally that the young are a threat and to assume that they are generally up to no good, and so in church we shy away from giving them the opportunity to lead or have responsibility for fear that something might go wrong or that we might be let down. We have a friend who encouraged his youth group to take a role in the leading of a service at the church. Included in the group was a young person who was not yet a Christian, but who wanted to be involved anyway. Tim, the youth worker, decided that a 'safe' option was to let him do the Bible reading. It was a scripted activity, surely nothing could go wrong? Halfway through the reading the young person stumbled on his words and rather than pausing to catch his breath and carry on, he swore loudly and started the reading again from the beginning. By contrast, Pete has been involved in a service where young people were allowed to read out prayers they had written. The language they used seemed very mature and on enquiry he discovered that the young people had submitted their prayers a week before the service, where they had been rewritten by an adult to make them more appropriate. For most of us the kind of mishap from Tim's experience is far preferable to the edited and sanitized involvement of Pete's experience, but for many the risks involved in allowing young people to get involved are just too great. Personally, we think the odd profanity could liven up many a service!

So what does it mean to be an adult in our world today? Look around at the world we access through our media, internet, the law and just how we interact with the people around us and we'll come across many signposts that indicate the point whereby you have entered 'adultland'. Clearly, the law has a lot to say about what we can do at what age, and if we are able to get married by sixteen, drive a car at seventeen and be a member of parliament and have a tequila sunrise in New York at twenty-one (preferably at the same time!) then our markers for maturity are clear. Or maybe not. Experience has told us, particularly in youth work, that these legal landmarks in our lives don't necessarily indicate becoming an adult and certainly, if we get things wrong during these significant years we are regularly reminded that adulthood is a destination way off on the horizon. When it comes to our own experience of 'growing up', how we are nurtured and raised plays a big part. Parental decisions and rules of the house vary from one family to the next, causing shouts from exasperated teenagers such as 'my mum's let me do that for years' to 'I'm not allowed to have my ears pierced till I'm thirty-six' coming from the corridors of our schools, shopping centres and churches. If our parents call the shots then do they make the final decision about when we become adults?

So when it comes to our faith and when we reach an adult state of belief – do we have those markers of maturity? When Jesus said we should have faith like a child, it's unlikely that he was suggesting that we should be immature, but to have what might be described as a faith that is simply and utterly dependent on God and trusting in him. That simple, dependent relationship with God would be a clear defining factor of being a mature Christian.

In our churches, do we have defined ideas of what it means to be an adult? Are we asking what it means to be spiritually mature?

Our own experiences would indicate that being an adult and having spiritual maturity are poles apart and research that we have already explored from Westerhoff and Fowler would indicate that too. Being an adult in the Church is easy, we just pack our diary to capacity with PCC meetings, flower arranging, cleaning rotas, reading the prayers, serving communion, making tea and coffee and being on the social committee. But if deep down we have no clear idea why we are doing it and, more importantly, who we are doing it for because we don't have a faith based on a relationship with God, then we are far from spiritual maturity. We're just really busy people.

As we've already mentioned in a previous chapter a spiritually mature person is described clearly in the confirmation service. Confirmation is about taking on an apostolic faith; 'continuing in the apostles' teaching and fellowship, in the breaking of bread and in prayers; persevering in resisting evil, and whenever falling into sin, repenting and returning to the Lord; proclaiming by word and example the good news of God in Christ; seeking and serving Christ in all people, loving one's neighbour as oneself; acknowledging Christ's authority over human society, praying for the world and its leaders, defending the weak and seeking peace and justice'. It's a very comprehensive picture. The mature Christian looks like someone who has been confirmed and who has taken upon themselves the words of the commission.

If we are searching for the ideal adult mature Christian then maybe we need to look back at our own faith journeys and ask the question: 'What marked our arrival into Christian adulthood?' The Church must play a significant part in how we might answer that question for ourselves and how we would possibly explore it with young people.

What marked your arrival into Christian adulthood? It would be a great question for young people to ask adults in their churches as they prepare for confirmation. Everyone's story is different. Here we would like to tell you our stories of what it meant for each of us becoming 'adult Christians'. Please humour us. We don't claim in any way to be spiritual giants, or the best examples of what spiritual maturity means, but rather as 'normal' Christians we feel that like so many others in our churches we have stories that young people will find encouraging and filled with hope.

Susie's Reflection

My own story, having made my entrance into church life via being a Gnome in the local church Brownie pack (Gnomes were one of the little groups within our pack – I really wanted to be a Pixie!), my experience of becoming an adult in the church was quite systematic, but in terms of becoming mature in my faith that's something very different. My earliest memories of church stem from when I went with my gran to her church in Sussex to help her with the flower arranging (I just watched, as from an early age it was clear that flower arranging wasn't something that I was gifted in), and I remember walking around, smelling the books, pretending I could play the organ and when adults came into the building being told to be quiet. I negotiated Sunday school and managed to convince my leaders that it was my birthday every three to four months landing me with a healthy stack of bookmarks and birthday cards (obviously way before child protection required us to have the essentials such as a date of birth on Sunday school registers). As I progressed through the subsequent youth groups I was made more aware of what I was expected to do in church, at what point in the service I was required to leave and when we could go back into the building after the service. Even when I went onto the PCC at the age of sixteen my presence and contributions seemed tokenistic and I felt completely unvalued.

However, almost simultaneously I was being mentored, pastored and discipled by some excellent youth leaders, I made a Christian commitment and began exploring ways to put my faith into action, including a desperate desire to go to Africa. You would imagine that confirmation would fit snugly into that journey but my day of wearing a posh dress and getting some lovely religious presents took place way before I began to put the pieces of my faith jigsaw together.

Someone else decided I was ready and that appears to resonate throughout our research on young people's experience of confirmation. Is it the case then that other people, as society already appears to be indicating, make the decision as to when we become an adult Christian? Do we decide when a person reaches Christian adulthood and is confirmation a response to that, a rite of passage to seal the deal?

Pete's Reflection

I didn't grow up in the Church, my grandma would take me to the Christingle service once a year in her local parish church, but that was the only time she or I went to church really. My parents didn't have me baptized when I was born; they wanted me to make my own mind up.

At the age of thirteen a series of events led my family (my mum, sister and myself) to start attending a local church. There we found acceptance and love. So we stayed, and in turn we each made commitments to Christ. I was confirmed shortly afterwards. As I've already hinted, my confirmation was an odd affair really.

I was prepared at school with my school chaplain, away from the church where I was growing and being discipled; my chaplain seemed to spend a lot of time trying to explain that the miracles weren't really miracles just coincidences, while my church was more of a 'six days of creation, means six periods of twenty-four hours' kind of place, so as you can imagine I was a little schizophrenic in my spiritual development.

Growing up as a Christian generally felt quite difficult for me. I was a classic 'Sunday Christian'; I was full of it when I was at church but the rest of the week I lived a life pretty indistinguishable from the rest of my friends at school. I was happy enough to talk about being a Christian, and indeed I tried to start a CU at school, but sadly I was certainly no paragon of virtue.

And that pretty much defines me for most of my Christian life. I avoided Christian Union at sixth form college, was president of the Student Christian Fellowship at university (I was the loudest at election time) and then I joined Youth for Christ.

Spiritual maturity for me has been realizing that there will come no magic moment when I will suddenly become 'spiritual'. Maturity for me is about doggedly keeping on with following Christ. I'm no great evangelist or prayer warrior – sometimes my prayer life seems rich and fulfilled, other times it feels like prayer is a dim and distant memory. I am happy to talk about my faith with my friends who aren't Christians, and I'm happy to invite them along to church events and so forth, but I'm unlikely to spend Saturdays preaching on street corners.

For me, maturity was the realization that I could think for myself about things of faith. It was a realization that I didn't have to agree with and believe whatever the preacher said. It was also the realization that I didn't have to agree with someone in order for us both to be right. I was fortunate enough to be able to do a masters degree a few years ago and at the first lecture Pete Ward, the course leader, asked each one of us in turn what salvation meant. We each gave different answers, we agreed on some points and on others we differed. The maturity that came was to realize that it didn't matter that we disagreed. We didn't have to try to convince each other of our individual points of view.

Can I say that the commission from the confirmation service is something I live out? Yes, a little. I've realized that God is involved in every aspect of my life. I can see him working and hear his voice in all things if I try. It means that I am aware of his presence and his leading in all things, whether it's buying washing powder or eating a meal. My hope is that with maturity has come a little peace, that I can be seen as someone who trusts in God, even if I don't have all the answers.

In our research with young people we asked whether 'being confirmed had made any differences in your life'. Many of them felt quite strongly that confirmation had marked an important step into having a mature faith. However, maturity of faith seemed to be split into two very clear areas. A lot of young people when asked how confirmation had changed them answered very much in personal terms – confirmation changed me and my attitudes:

> '. . . it's helped me stop putting myself first and leading life my own way . . .'

> '. . . it made me be more confident to talk about Christianity to friends and family . . .'

> '. . . I feel calmer and lighter as a person . . .'

> '. . . it made me more dedicated to reading my Bible and praying . . .'

In fact, of the 142 people who answered the question 'Why did you get confirmed?' 23 said that it was about a 'next step' in their faith, or 'moving on with God' in some way, and 58 talked about confirmation being a public confirmation of their personal faith.

For these young people, maturity of faith is marked by personal or internal factors. For them their faith is marked by what's going on inside, and by the personal commitments that they have made.

Other young people answered the same question by sharing how being confirmed had affected their place within their community. For them, maturity of faith was marked by their place within the Church:

> '. . . a feeling of belonging in the Church . . .'

> '. . . I can now do more in the C of E . . .'

> '. . . [I] feel a part of, and stakeholder in, the C of E . . .'

> '. . . it was a real sign of my belonging to the C of E . . .'

Fifteen of the young people who answered the questionnaire felt that they got confirmed to mark that they now belonged to the Church or to mark their 'commitment to Anglican Christianity'.

Interestingly, it would appear that these groups can be split by the churchmanship of the confirming church. The young people who felt that maturity of faith was rooted in their personal growth and experience generally came from an evangelical background and the young people who felt that maturity was about their place in the community came from a more high church setting. While both factors are important and maturity can be measured by both, it is a useful warning to us to recognize if our teaching leans too far one way or another. Young people need both elements of the picture in order to be mature Christians; a stronger understanding of what it means to be a Christian personally and a clearer view of what their role and place within the community needs to become.

Many young people in our churches may well relate to the young priest in the film *Chocolat* who comes to his new parish only to have each and every one of his sermons taken by Alfred Molina's character, the Comte de Reynaud, and rewritten. His frustration with the well-meaning, but ultimately patronizing adult who consistently undermines the young priest's work and crushes the calling that God has placed on his life is palpable. At the end of the film, where the priest is eventually given the opportunity to speak without the interference from the Comte, his simple and grace-filled sermon proves to contain more power and more life-changing truth than any of the judgemental or complicated words from the Comte.

The truth is, as we've already acknowledged, that when we give young people leadership roles in church settings we often are taking risks; you will remember the young man who punctuated a Scripture reading with an expletive.

But while allowing young people to lead in the church occasionally ends up with things not going quite to plan, the story is often the complete opposite. Often when young people lead, either in a worship setting or in any other church setting we discover in them something truly fresh and exciting. Just as in *Chocolat*, when we allow a young person to speak from their heart, to lead with the word that they have received from God, we as adults can learn and develop in amazing ways.

Susie's reflection

In a parish that will, understandably, remain nameless, I was chatting with some members of the church about confirmation and the young people in their church. As they explained how it worked in their church, the confirmation preparation course that the young people undertook and the pomp and ceremony of the confirmation service, they proceeded to tell me, with great enthusiasm, that once the young people were confirmed they were '*allowed* to collect empty coffee cups after the morning services'. It must have taken every muscle in my body to stop shaking and make some kind of innocuous response and back quite rapidly away from the conversation, make my way to the car park and shout 'WHAAAAT!'

But way up the other end of the spectrum, I've experienced the empowering of young people in a parish where they have been so involved in the work of the church that the line between adult and child maturity is very faint. This particular parish encouraged young people in teaching, preaching, leading, planning, worship, being on the PCC and having an authentic voice, evangelism, social action and so much more. And that expression of authentic value towards the young people made confirmation more of a response to where the young people were at in their spiritual lives than a procedure for putting young people into the spiritual category they should be in according to the church.

Pete's reflection

One of the churches in The Diocese of Winchester offered the young people the chance to be in small groups and to lead themselves – to decide what they wanted to do in their time together. Two groups in particular really stood out to me because of the choices they made when given the opportunity to lead. One group, a group of young men, decided that as well as meeting for prayer and Bible study as intended they would meet together to jam. They were all guitar players and so decided that every so often they would meet simply to play guitar – they would all plug in and jam. A second group of young women, again met for their regular sessions of prayer and so on, but also decided that they wanted to do something active for their community. Given the opportunity to choose to do any activity, they approached a local care home and visited the elderly folk there regularly.

You see while young people sometimes surprise us with their actions in a negative way, we can often find ourselves surprised by young people in an altogether positive way. Time and again while working in a local parish I would give young people the option to lead or be involved in leading a service at church. I know that when adults came to what the young people had planned, more often than not they would come expecting something akin to a rock concert, and while the young people would often choose loud music, the themes for the services they ran were generally quiet and reflective. Time after time adults would leave the services that the young people had planned and led surprised by how creative and contemplative the young people were.

The point is simple really. If confirmation is an acknowledgement that young people have made an adult decision for faith then as the Church we must treat them as adults once they have made that stand. Imagine how it must feel as a young person to be told that by being confirmed you are standing up and deciding for yourself that you want to be a Christian, making that decision and the incredibly brave action of saying the words – being blessed by the bishop and so on – and then discovering that it makes absolutely no difference to the way you are treated. It's no surprise then that so many young people leave church shortly after confirmation. If the truth be told we need to be ready to treat young people as adults whether or not they choose confirmation, but the point still stands.

And while confirmation only marks one step along the road of discipleship, it must surely make a difference. It must surely mark the point where we help a young person to discover what true mature faith looks like. In Ephesians 4.15 we are told that we must '. . . grow up into him who is the Head, that is Christ'. Confirmation can and should be a point to mark our becoming more like Jesus.

For Jesus, that moment of moving into maturity occurred shortly after his thirteenth birthday as he sat in the Temple courts listening to the teachers and asking them questions. If we refuse to afford young people the opportunity to speak as mature members of our communities, if we don't allow them to sit among the elders to speak and ask questions, if we hurry them away to get on with colouring while we adults go about the job of being proper Christians, then we run the risk of missing the very voice of Jesus.

Finally, it is of utmost importance that we must remain vigilant with the language we use when encouraging young people to take up positions of maturity and responsibility within our churches. There is no doubt that what people say to us sticks – especially when the words they choose to use drag us down from the sunshine on the mountain top to the valleys of despondency. We'll all remember times when we have been inspired, motivated and encouraged by affirming and empowering words, and equally we know the effect of patronizing and devaluing words. If we are with our young people on their journey of faith, whatever route that takes us, and encouraging them to grow, but our language and our actions don't replicate that, then we are in danger of causing confusion and despondency.

Susie's reflection

An example of this is when a vicar mentioned to me once that he would like the young people to get involved in church services but was very clear that he was '*allowing*' and '*letting*' the young people participate. When I challenged him on his use of language (which may I say went down *really* well) he explained that the young people had to do what he said and he didn't want anything that was going to upset the congregation. I'd rather he used that language in conversation with me than with his young people, but really, I'd rather he didn't use it at all. Give young people an opportunity to bring all that they have to offer to the church, but restrict them with disempowering language and unnecessary guidelines, and we invite them purely to colour within the lines with crayons that we've selected for them. It's far better that we give them a blank piece of paper and tell them to go for it, while we sit back and enjoy.

Some suggestions for putting this chapter into practice

- Put your young people in positions where they can make genuine decisions and where their decisions will make a real difference to the church. This may mean encouraging them to stand for election to the PCC, or other committees involved in the planning and running of the church.

- Give them opportunities to plan and lead the worship in the church. We are often asked to go to churches and to help groups plan their first ever youth service. Often the leaders of the groups understand this to mean that they plan the service and give young people jobs to do in it. What we tend to do is to get the young people to discuss what worship is, from a biblical perspective. We then thrash out what we think worship has to have and what is periphery. With those things in mind we then simply ask the young people what they want to do. That seems like good discipleship, there has been teaching and direction, but the young people then get to take that teaching and apply it for themselves.

- Give them the cheque book. Give them a bunch of cash and see what they do with it.

- Take the commission from the confirmation seriously, help young people to work out what living out those promises might look like and then look at ways of making space for that to happen in your church.

There are some further ideas in Chapter 10 where we explore what to do with groups post-confirmation.

Chapter 8

Confirmation Preparation

Over many years our experiences of preparing for confirmation will have spanned countless venues, personnel, resources, times and so on, but what remains the same, utterly unchangeable, is the need to undertake a process of discovering and understanding the foundational elements of the Christian faith before the bishop can lay his hands on your head. So welcome to this chapter, one that will explore the ways in which we prepare young people for confirmation, looking at how we do this, when we do this, and what resources we use, as well as addressing and grappling with deeper thinking around our approach, our motivation and considering the possibility of changing the 'way we've always done it'.

Susie's reflection

As you'll have gathered by now, much of my own confirmation process was absorbed with admiring the lovely Toby. I'm sure I must have taken some of the teaching in – I'm sure that we had some fun as a group, and I do remember reading the chapters of the book when we were asked to. I also remember that the curate who led our confirmation class was incredibly energetic and I knew then and I think I still know now that he was deeply committed to us as a group of young people and in what he was teaching . . . even if I can't remember a whole lot of it.

Confirmation preparation has been a varied experience for us. We have been involved in preparing a large number of young people for confirmation over the years in our different incarnations of youth work. Those occasions have remained embedded in our minds and in our hearts for a number of reasons.

Susie's reflection

Some occasions stand out because they resulted in large quantities of laughter and some embarrassing situations. There was the time when we took a group of young people to a residential centre in the south of the country and had a packed weekend full of teaching, fun and all the other stuff that is wrapped up in time away. Our teaching sessions, and chilling sessions and, well, pretty much the whole weekend was punctuated by the warden of the residential centre pressing her face up against the window of the room, just watching us in an eerie and peculiar way. We did enquire as to whether she needed something or whether, indeed, she wanted to join us, but she would scuttle away as quickly as she had appeared. We never used that place again! There was also the time when we were leading a group in preparation for confirmation in the church building on a very hot, sunny day. We decided to take the brand new chairs from the church out onto the newly refurbished entrance balcony which had recently been 'tarmac'ed. We finished the session, which I clearly remember was on Church, and as we got up to leave, none of us could. We were embedded in the church veranda. Our chairs had sunk in to the warm tarmac. You may be thinking 'that's comical but how does it make a difference to confirmation preparation?' I'm convinced that the relationships that we had with each other and the atmosphere we created made those situations as memorable as they are. We were relaxed enough to laugh with and at each other. It made a difference and we'll talk more about relationships later in the chapter.

Some occasions stand out more than others: sometimes because of the change in the lives of the young people that we worked with; sometimes because of the questions that they asked, which not only helped to clarify their own faith but had a deep impact on our own. Above all though is the joy found in seeing a young person grow through the experience of confirmation, and then staying the course beyond the service rather than seeing it as a passing out parade. As we have already explored, it's not every young person that completes confirmation and then carries on in their faith.

Structure

The stereotypical picture of a group of young people sitting in the vicar's study or lounge is one that we come across often and we are sure that this preparation venue and structure still exists today in many churches around the country. In our research we asked 138 people whether the person who prepared them for confirmation was ordained: 100 of them answered yes, that's 72 per cent. We asked the same people specifically who it was that prepared them: 69 per cent of our respondents said that their vicar or chaplain prepared them, 34 per cent their youth leader and 1 per cent their teacher – which seems to bear that assumption out.

As well as this more traditional picture of preparation, we are increasingly coming across new and innovative methods of confirmation preparation; some of these are different in terms of when the preparation takes place and others are more creative in respect of who leads it.

Let's unpack first the structure of different methods of preparing young people for confirmation.

The 'traditional' method

Perhaps the most common method of preparing young people for confirmation is the weekly session over a period of anything from a couple of months up to a year. This group is usually run by a clergy person. These can be really useful sessions. Taking a subject each week and linking them closely together over regular meetings can help to build the big picture for the group of what it means to be confirmed, what their faith is about and what they do with their faith from this point onwards. Their regularity promotes good relationships both between the leaders and the young people and between the young people themselves.

Susie's reflection

I was involved in a confirmation preparation course that met on a monthly basis on Saturdays. The preparation took place over four months, so on each of the Saturdays that we met we would cover at least three or four subject areas. As with the weekly confirmation class I was involved in, there was a very high expectation on the young people that they would be there every month as well as attending church each week too. If any of the young people missed a session it was a big deal and if 'homework' was set then there was an expectation on them to do it even if they hadn't attended the session that related to the 'homework'. For the young people the Saturday proved to be a struggle due to other activities that they were involved in, along with family commitments and holidays, and there wasn't any room for renegotiating the time. This was set and the expectation was that 'if they wanted to be confirmed then they had to come to the classes and that's when they were'. My concern was that this model didn't take onboard the world of the young person and their families, an issue that was more apparent with the young people who were not from Christian families. And while it is not possible to create a course that fits each individual personally, shouldn't we consider the bigger picture of their lives and balance that with this key time of learning, understanding and growing?

It is right to assume that the person leading the preparation has important information to share with the young people on the course, but that cannot be at the expense of the leader viewing themselves as a fellow traveller. The young people will have come to their preparation with needs and with questions, and if what we have prepared is so rigid that it allows no room for them to explore issues for themselves and, critically, to ask questions, then we are doing them a great disservice.

Furthermore (and we'll talk more about this in Chapter 10 about what happens post-confirmation), what we do has to be sustainable. The young person's discipleship doesn't end on the day of confirmation. Our preparation must take into account what we plan to do for the young people after the service.

Susie's reflection

I once asked a vicar who was running a confirmation preparation group what he planned to run for this group of over twenty young people once they had been confirmed. I was stunned by the reply: 'They don't need anything after they are confirmed.' After I scraped myself off the floor and made my way home, I just felt a profound sadness that these young people had been meeting together for confirmation preparation over a number of months, they had been growing and learning and preparing for this great event and then there would be . . . nothing . . . zilch.

If we have a structure of confirmation preparation that fits a young person's world and becomes something that is part of their life, we should, we believe, do all we can to sustain that journey beyond the confirmation service. Whether that is through integrating the young people into an existing youth group, by setting up a brand new group, or by getting together with another group from another church and meeting regularly with them.

The residential

Then there is the weekend away. If you've spent any time exploring the benefits of residentials and come to the conclusion that they are a hugely beneficial time and key element of your youth work, you'll most probably have explored the possibilities of doing confirmation preparation over a weekend. Now some who are very specific about the areas that the young people cover in their preparation might pose an immediate objection – can we fit all elements of transubstantiation and the exploration of predestination among sessions on church, the Bible, prayer and the late night game of Unihoc and continual eating of Haribo? That's a question we can't answer unfortunately (although it certainly sounds like a jolly good weekend!), but what we can say from personal experience is that getting to grips with some of these core areas of what it means to be a Christian and live the Christian life can fit into a weekend thoroughly and creatively . . . even if you have to shave a bit off your transubstantiation!

Susie's reflection

Residentials are such a great part of our work with young people. I love them because we get away from the fast pace of life and get an opportunity to press pause. Its been my experience that in these times young people give themselves the chance to explore more of who God is, what he has done and is doing, and how that impacts their own individual lives. The practicalities of eating with each other, not having a 'pick up time' at the end of the evening meaning that time isn't really that important (apart from still being awake at 3.30am!), having space to be alone but also having time to spend with each other, and maybe even the leaders. It's just great and one of my very favourite elements of youth ministry, so it made sense to use a residential as a place for confirmation preparation.

Because the weekend created a bit more space, on the one
that we ran we found ourselves with time to talk more
about the subject areas, deal with and explore questions
and issues that came out for the group as a whole or
individuals, and we had time to pray for each other without
the worry that the parents would be waiting outside in
their cars if we over-ran. And, if I need to sell this structure
of preparation to you any further, even today, many years
later, the young people who were on that weekend still
recall the eating, the lack of sleeping, the fun and games,
the spiders in the kitchen cupboard, and the teaching, the
growing, the understanding and the changing.

If you like the idea of taking your youth group away for a weekend to
help them prepare for confirmation, then you'll love what the
Evangelical Lutheran Church of Finland do.

The Finnish model (Susie's reflection)

It's been a huge privilege to be involved in a very different type of
confirmation preparation since I started my post as Diocesan Youth
Officer for the Diocese of Manchester. The diocese has enjoyed a good
and prosperous relationship with the Diocese of Tampere in the
Evangelical Lutheran Church of Finland and as part of that relationship
the previous Youth Officer of the Diocese of Manchester explored,
along with the Finnish youth leaders, chaplains and church leaders how
they 'did' confirmation preparation. Before we launch into the unique
and exciting ways in which the Evangelical Lutheran Church of Finland
do confirmation, its necessary to make clear that confirmation is very
much part of the rite of passage for those who live in Finland and other
Scandinavian countries. For example, in order to be married in church
you need to be confirmed. It's different from the way things are in the
UK. For the Finns there is a greater emphasis on confirmation because,
understandably, more people want to do it. While for some it may well

be a legalistic hoop they feel they have to jump through, that certainly isn't the case for all. Even with this in mind, their approach is well worth a mention.

The preparation of young people for confirmation in the Evangelical Lutheran Church of Finland (ELCF) takes pride of place within the youth work of the church. Although they do offer the option to undertake confirmation preparation in weekly meetings, nine out of ten young people opt for the confirmation camp model. The camp model is based on several meetings during the early part of the year which create the opportunity to get to know the young people, as the leaders of the camp aren't necessarily from the parish that the young people come from, and also provides an occasion for some fun and social activities. The main camp which takes place during the summer lasts for seven days and involves an extensive amount of teaching with worship, reflection, sports, entertainment and plenty of eating (we had five meals each day when we visited a Finnish confirmation camp in the summer of 2009).

And it appears to work.

In 2007, 59,888 young people underwent confirmation preparation in Finland and 47,573 made the choice to do their preparation on a camp. 88.5 per cent of these young people are fifteen years old and this yearly total is on the increase. You might just need a moment to absorb those figures. Our ministry certainly isn't about numbers but you would have to agree that this is a huge amount of young people in one year.[1]

We can now appreciate a little more as to why this is the jewel in the crown of the ELCF; this is a significant, growing and life-changing ministry in the Finnish church.

It's important at this stage to unpack how confirmation sits in the lives of Finnish people. It is a key part of the overall ministry of the church and in a recent parish employee survey 82 per cent of church employees regarded confirmation as 'a very important field of work'.[2] If we step back into the history of confirmation in Finland we can also see how important being confirmed was for individuals as members of society. In the past if you hadn't been confirmed, drinking alcohol and coffee, and smoking were not allowed. After confirmation these things were allowed, and girls were permitted to wear their hair up, boys could wear shirts and a young person could then 'court members of the opposite sex and assume responsibilities'.[3] So being confirmed has huge significance as part of growing up and has stood as 'the' rite of passage for Finnish young people. Naturally, over time these conditions have changed, but in order for you to take the bread and wine at communion, become a godparent and be married in a church in Finland, you must still be confirmed. I suspect that some of you are concluding that being married could be fairly high on the agenda of Finnish young people so that must be why so many go through the confirmation process and I think that there must be some truth in that, but having been part of the preparation and delivery of a Finnish confirmation camp, I'm convinced that there is more to it than that. From those I spoke to there seemed to be a clear understanding of the relevance and purpose of confirmation as a key part of their growth as a Christian. There was the opportunity to 'ask the important questions' and having space to talk openly about issues that the young people brought to the table were hugely beneficial. This is a key part of the structure of preparation; asking questions and investing in shared learning; talking together and not just 'listening all the time' (ref: almost every young person I've met!). We may well give space for questions at the end of each session, but those can very often be 'tag-ons' and without the time to do justice to both the question and the answer. Giving more time to the thinking of our young people can be valuable for all involved; providing regular opportunities for questions with enough time to explore them speaks value to our young people and gives us insight into their journey and can and has been revelational in terms of our own faith.

One of the other key dimensions of the Finnish camp model of confirmation preparation is the role of the Young Confirmed Volunteer (YCV). The role of the YCV is to take on the responsibility of an assistant leader in the confirmation preparation of other young people, whether that is on a camp or in regular lessons, and to support the ongoing children's and youth work of the parish. In K. Tirri's paper 'The History of Young Confirmed Voluntary Workers in Finland', she goes as far as to claim that part of the success of the confirmation camp model is down to the role of the YCVs and reflects on Turunen's point from Tulevaisuuden Rippikoulu (The future of confirmation education,1997) that the ministry of YCVs is one of the most important lay ministries of the Evangelical Lutheran Church of Finland.[4]

Tirri states that 'in essence, YCV activity is about how youth, a few years older, can support younger youth to grow in the direction defined in . the CTP 2001,'[5] this being that 'young people, having received through Holy Baptism a faith in the triune God, should be reinforced in this faith; that they should grow in their love for their fellow human beings, and live a life of prayer in communion with the congregation'.[6]

In 2007 we are greeted again with more encouraging figures that underpin the value of the Finnish model of confirmation; a total of 27,000 young people attended the training to become YCVs and a total of 18,000 young people worked as young confirmed volunteers. Until I had the opportunity to be part of a Finnish Confirmation Camp, I was unaware of how pivotal the role of the YCVs is and for the duration of the week they seemed to be constantly involved in leading small groups, entertaining and running games and sports. A couple of those from the camp I was on had only been confirmed the year before and were keen to be involved again in an experience which had obviously been life shaping for them. The only problematic factor in this area is that as you can well imagine there are often too many YCVs for the roles (excuse me . . . too many volunteers?) and the camps, so there are some who are left out. Tirri states that this is a tricky situation and how the church continues to motivate and value those who are not given a role is worthy of further investigation.

Just before we leave the Finnish model one final figure from 2007; while the vast majority of those 59,888 young people who were confirmed were already church members, as a result of the confirmation camps, a further 1,859, having undertaken confirmation preparation, joined the church. The ELCF are naturally thrilled that through this vital part of their ministry young people are just *beginning* to explore who God is, what the cross means to them, and all the other elements of the Christian faith through confirmation preparation, so it seems to me that there isn't a faith criterion to meet before that preparation starts. Come as you are and see what happens – a missional and evangelistic approach to confirmation that maybe others might not be so comfortable with. Have we decided that in order for people to be confirmed they have to meet a certain check list of spirituality and knowledge before they can embark on their preparation? The question of 'are you ready?' isn't always addressed honestly to the young person as a direct question, but sits there as an assumption like the proverbial elephant in the room accompanied by a slight anxiety that something utterly terrible might just happen if this young person begins the confirmation journey in an 'unready' state.

St Laurence's, Chorley (Susie's reflection)

One church with which I have worked were willing to totally rethink the way they prepared young people for confirmation. They saw that a separate course that ended with the confirmation service had weaknesses and were willing to try a whole new approach.

And before we go any further with this story please acclimatize yourself to the word 'change'. It appears a lot and for many of us it's not a word that we might naturally use when it comes to talking about processes within the church that have been the same for years – and years.

The parish of St Laurence, based in the town of Chorley, Lancashire is a key church in the town and the vicar of the parish plays a significant role not just within the church but is highly respected within the local community and the surrounding area. The average congregation each Sunday is around 250 with a Sunday school and young people's activities taking place on both Sunday mornings and Sunday evenings. The groups are well attended and there is a committed body of leaders and helpers for all of the age ranges.

In order to understand the change that they made it's key for us to unpack how they used to do things when it came to confirmation. The key age range for confirmation at St Laurence's is around eleven and twelve years old. Each Sunday evening two groups would meet; a pre-confirmation group whose sole purpose was to prepare candidates for confirmation and a post-confirmation group who had some games, some Bible teaching and generally hung out. It is important to note that these two groups were very distinctive in when they met and how they viewed each other. If you were confirmed then you didn't mix with those who hadn't been confirmed.

Each year the pre-confirmation group was well attended. I would love to say that this was due to a large number of young people eagerly wishing to explore more of the Christian faith and ultimately make a public declaration of their faith a few months later. However, this would not exactly be the case for this church and many other churches in this country. Many of the young people who came to do confirmation preparation and ultimately got confirmed were there because of their and/or their parents' desire to get them into the local Church of England high school – a story that many of us can relate to in our parishes.

At the beginning of their confirmation preparation time you could tell those who were there because of the 'school' factor and those who were there with a genuine desire to explore faith.

The pre-confirmation group would meet each Sunday, tuck away a couple of packets of chocolate biscuits and some fizzy drinks, and look at a particular element of the Christian faith. These sessions were regularly led by the curate or the vicar who were and still are a very positive element in the confirmation preparation. As the confirmation date approached, the excitement for the event was tangible, the outfits and presents were being bought and the rehearsals began to take place, but somewhere in the midst of the sense of enthusiasm there was a very different type of anticipation beginning to be expressed.

As the leaders and clergy looked ahead to this momentous service for these young people there was a very clear feeling of sadness. They knew that this could very possibly be the last time that they saw the majority of the group of young people, knowing that this experience of preparing for confirmation and the actual service would spell the end of these young people coming to church. The allure of a post confirmation group was not huge due to the 'them and us' attitude felt among many of the young people and the roles that some post-confirmation young people would take on, such as becoming servers for the morning Holy Communion service, as a result of being confirmed, were not for everyone.

The church had become aware that because of the process they used to prepare young people for confirmation, they were setting themselves up to fail when it came to maintaining relationships with the young people after the confirmation service. As a church they wanted to do something about it. They had realized that it was the very nature of the process that they had delivered over the years that needed to be addressed.

And with the help of some external folk, that is exactly what they did.

Allow me to go off on a tangent. We can all be very sensitive and super protective of the ways in which we do things. 'We've always done things this way and it's worked (to an extent) and so there is no need to change. Please don't challenge me to change what I do because then I look like I've failed and people will think that I'm no good anymore and when the new ideas come in I'll have to do something that someone else has told me to do and secretly wish I'd had the idea in the first place.' We've become a little (or dare I say quite a bit) paranoid. As we look at the positives of what we are doing, even if they are far outweighed by the negatives, we cling on for dear life to what we believe to be the right way when actually we are desperately trying to ignore the signs facing us that say it's not working anymore. We've all been there and we know what it does to our self esteem.

So it is a brave step to go through that emotional rollercoaster and still see the potential that change can bring.

Now I'm not suggesting that this church went through a particularly emotional and negative time as they reviewed their process, but with change comes change, and that doesn't always go down too well with everyone.

Conversations were had with a variety of people with varying degrees of experience of confirmation and working with young people. Consultations took place among the youth leaders and clergy, and a new strategy of how the church could do confirmation began to emerge. The whole emphasis of a preparation course with a defined end was being challenged and a keenness to weave the preparation for confirmation into the ongoing youth work and discipleship of young people was being voiced. This inevitably meant that the youth groups as they stood would be restructured and instead of two different youth groups with two different purposes, there would be one group for eleven to fourteen year-olds. They would still have a lot of fun, eat a lot of chocolate biscuits and drink fizzy drinks. Furthermore, they would still take a core element of the Christian faith and seek to understand it further. For those who were being confirmed it still provided what the church felt they needed to know and for those who had already been confirmed it provided an opportunity to revisit a subject in order to understand it further and from different perspectives. The hope was and continues to be that these young people will not know the process of confirmation as a beginning, middle and end, but as a key part of the jigsaw of exploring who they are in Christ and how the Christian faith can impact the rest of their lives.

Joan, one of the volunteer youth leaders, says this:

> I thank God for those youngsters who do decide to go ahead and be confirmed but maybe I thank him more for those who are brave enough to say 'I'm not ready right now' or 'I want to wait.' Standing against your peers and what is expected is never easy and demands a respect in its own right. I know that, at least for these youngsters, the choice they make is real and well considered. It is often family expectation that is hardest to cope

with and while we would not encourage a child to disobey parents we would offer them every support and offer to talk with their family too. About three months before confirmation is scheduled we ask the children to write down their reasons why they want to be confirmed. This is always an exercise done anonymously and has always proved beneficial and eye-opening. Their reasons vary: 'It will help me follow Jesus and God better', 'It will help me be a better person', 'I don't know why – but I just want to', 'I want to taste the bread and the wine', 'my mum says I have to', 'I can have a new outfit', 'because I was baptized', 'my brother was done last year and it's my turn now.'

Once they are confirmed, well, they get their presents and wear a new outfit and get a picture with the bishop and then the following Sunday they are back at youth club, because for the vast majority nothing has changed about Sunday nights. It's still Sunday night, still youth club and we'll still keep looking at key elements of the Christian faith.

Joan continues:

> We teach that following Christ is a lifestyle and not just for Sunday. Consequently we do not run a confirmation class but cover all topics in the two or more years the youngsters are with us in Pathfinders, after which we feed them into the next age youth group. Our meetings start with the 6.00pm Informal Eucharist and finish at 7.45pm. We cater for those in academic years 6 and 7. This also used to include year 8 too but increased numbers have been one cause of change. Meetings consist of teaching, games, activities, walks, eating together and present many opportunities to talk; our Christian faith is perhaps caught better than it is taught and this means that as leaders we need not only to be honest with the youngsters we serve but vulnerable in a way too. They catch how we act and react, personal integrity is so important.
>
> While we follow the lectionary for the basis of our curriculum, this is explored and expressed in many ways and many different

tools are used by the team who lead the group. A Simpsons DVD (with obligatory donuts), agape meal, craft sessions, visits out – local music centre, a monastery, summer walks and picnics across the holidays. Each leader uses the medium they are comfortable with, supported by the rest of the team.

If we communicate an ending then we can expect people to leave; we have already explored that at some length in a previous chapter. If we communicate that there is still so much more to come, then by and large people will want to know what that is. If we embed our confirmation preparation in the ongoing work to engage our young people with the good news of the risen Christ, then this story from St Laurence's, Chorley and other stories of change from around the country, may mean that we see our young people carrying on in their faith, turning up at church or youth group not wanting an end but wanting more.

Content

It's rather difficult to recommend a confirmation preparation course because there is so little written specifically for the purpose. There are, however, plenty of courses out there that will help exploration of some of the basics of the Christian faith. We have included an Appendix with a selection of the courses that are currently in print and some of the things they contain and what we recommend from each.

Needless to say, the best course is the one that you have pulled together specifically for your group, taking the best from all the resources at your disposal. Writing a course from scratch is hard work, but rewarding.

Susie's reflection

I found myself in the slightly unusual situation of having to prepare a whole confirmation course from scratch without any of my usual, reliable resources and needed to do it in the space of a week. I sat with a pad of paper, one book and my Bible. I felt daunted and stressed by the situation I was in, but as I worked out the issues to cover, the key points in each of those issues and things that have helped me to understand them, it came together. Certainly, without question, the Holy Spirit played a huge part in putting this last minute course together, and others around who delivered sessions were invaluable, but I couldn't have imagined the outcome. We had some great discussions, some differences of opinion, thought-provoking questions and moments of clarity – it was great and I'm so thankful to God for his divine intervention. But something happened that I hadn't bargained on – I found myself going back to the basics for myself and exploring again the staples of my relationship with God, and it was so, so good to be renewed in my faith and be reminded what brought me to the point of choosing to follow Jesus. It's not indulgent for us to travel the journey with our young people and give ourselves time to reaffirm our faith.[7]

Who leads the preparation?

It isn't just the content of the preparation that we need to think through very carefully. You will remember we discovered both from our experience and from the research we did that the majority of confirmation candidates are prepared by an ordained person – usually the vicar of their church. In Chapter 6 exploring why confirmation is often seen as a passing out parade we were at pains to point out that we see no issue with that.

What would be a shame was if it was assumed that the vicar should do the preparation as a matter of course; if for some reason it was felt that confirmation preparation was exclusively the domain of the clergy.

We would argue that whoever prepares the young person for confirmation needs to be willing to go the long haul. It can be damaging for a young person if they feel that they only warrant the attention from the clergy when they are preparing for this moment of their lives, and it can be pretty dispiriting for the regular youth leaders if they feel that somehow they aren't up to scratch for this particular task.

In a church where the youth work is led by paid staff or volunteers, confirmation preparation is a great opportunity for the clergy to work *with* those people – to learn from each other and to journey together even if it's just for a short while.

Looking at ourselves

Before we draw this chapter to a close let's finish by stepping back and taking a look at ourselves and thinking through some slightly challenging questions.

In preparing these amazing young people for confirmation, for this point where they stand in front of a large number of people and make promises and commitments about their relationship with God and maybe even have the chance to share that with the congregation, we need to be sure that we are utterly committed to what we are teaching them. If we believe what we are telling young people about the core elements of what it means to be a follower of God with determination, passion and commitment, that makes a huge difference. If we bring who we are in Christ, our experiences and understandings to what we teach and discuss with young people, then we bring a whole new dimension to what could be a dreary old session. At the beginning of the chapter Susie mentioned that she didn't remember much about the actual content of her confirmation preparation classes, but what she does remember is the energy with which it was delivered. It's the passion that Susie's curate had for what he was teaching and the stories of his own Christian life that made an impact on her life. Susie couldn't pinpoint a particular session or story, but she knows that her preparation experience gave her something from somebody with passion and energy that was worth pursuing, worth following, worth believing in.

Let not our confirmation preparation become a regular, mundane thing that we do at a certain time each year, rolling out the same old material that's 'worked before so will work again' (and what does 'work' mean in this context anyway?), and approaching it with a less than exuberant spirit and with a matter of fact mentality. This is life-changing stuff that once changed *our* lives, and should *keep* changing our lives, and we have this tremendous privilege to share it with young people so that they might know that same life-changing work of God.

Susie's reflection

I know a youth leader in Manchester who wanted to run a session on the nature of God. He wanted to communicate to the young people the enormity and awesomeness of our Creator. Rather than talk about this great God while sitting on their chairs in the youth club he took the young people to a road at the end of the runway at Manchester airport (not *in* the airport) and sat watching the planes take off. If you're *that* close to the plane as it takes off, your whole body is shaken by the power of that huge metal beast as it roars up into the sky, defying the very laws of gravity. It connects with every single one of your senses. The youth worker explained to the young people that even with all of their senses overwhelmed, that experience couldn't touch what it must be like to sit in the presence of the living God.

It would have been so much easier to stay in the safety and warmth of the church hall, much like it would be easier for us to continue delivering the confirmation preparation as we have always done it. But when we are talking about helping our young people connect with God then it has to be worth us pushing the boat out.

If we are ready to look at how we prepare young people for confirmation in a fresh and, dare I say, alternative way then let's not limit the possibilities of making this a significant and memorable time for them. I'm not looking for personal satisfaction, knowing that I did a great job, I ticked the list of all the subjects I should cover and the young people were generally smiling . . . I'm looking for space for all of us to explore and be transformed by who God is and what he has done for us. Make this an adventure – if you have a session to plan on creation why not abandon the church hall and head up your nearest hill or mountain and talk about it there.

Go on . . . why not? They'll never forget it.

Chapter 9

The Confirmation Service

The confirmation service is the pinnacle of the confirmation process. It marks weeks, months or maybe even years of preparation and it's the symbolic moment at which all that we have talked about is put into action. We've already agreed that it's not the end of the journey, but rather it's the next step or the start of a new leg.

We have lost count of how many young people have told us that it was at the point of confirmation that everything slotted into place for them spiritually and in terms of their discipleship. For many it seems to mark the point when they took their faith seriously, a real make or break moment.

For most people the confirmation service is the first time that they get the chance to get up close and personal with the bishop. In fact for many, it might be the only time that they sit or stand face to face with the symbolic head of their diocese and for lots of us the moment carries something of a celebrity moment.

Bishops guard their confirmation services jealously. Confirmation can't happen without the bishop and so the bishops tend to take the occasions very seriously, so it seemed only sensible to call in the experts as we wrote this chapter.

Paul Butler is the Bishop of Nottingham and Southwell, although when we spoke to him he had just finished as the Bishop of Southampton. He is also the Archbishop's Advocate for Children. Mark Davies is the Bishop of Middleton. What follows is the transcript of conversations we had with them during the Spring of 2010.

We started by asking them about their most enjoyable confirmation services of the past twelve months.

+Mark: This is not ducking out, but I would say that every confirmation service is memorable because for those people it's only going to happen once. I may have a confirmation service four times a week, but they have only got one in a lifetime and so I'm very conscious that each time this is a unique opportunity to engage with those people at a profound level, share with them in the most tremendous gift. Every one of them is special.

+Paul: All confirmations stand out in different ways. One or two would be more distinctive than others. I did an evening confirmation at St James' Church in Shirley which included some baptisms by full immersion as well as the confirmation. Young people and adults, a real mix of ages, and very informal in style.

Was it the informality that made it distinctive?

+Paul: Yes, and the age range. The most recent one I did was at East Dene; the smallest place that I've got virtually in my patch, it's a classic small rural community, a vicar looking after the four churches in his benefice and just in a quiet way seeing people coming to faith and growing in faith. At this service there were just three people being confirmed from a village of about 250 people. What was significant about that was that it was a mum and a son and then another young person. I confirmed the mum's oldest son three years ago at Hampshire Collegiate School in a school-based confirmation and as part of her testimony she said that it was her son being confirmed three years ago that made her think about wanting to get more involved. Often the significance that I get is the stories that I hear from people.

+Mark: I will always remember my first confirmation service because it was a man who was dying and he was looking to be confirmed in the August and I was ordained a bishop in the April. His parish priest phoned and said that he wouldn't live until August and he was very sorry about not being confirmed. So on the Monday I went to his home and confirmed him and his wife. (Bishop Mark points to a picture of the event on his mantelpiece). His family, including young grandchildren, were all present and talking to them afterwards and since the grandfather's death, it became apparent that the confirmation of their granddad had made a huge impact on them. So every confirmation is special, every one is precious and they are all different, which is an amazing thing really because we use the same liturgy for each one and yet each one feels so different. So for me they are all very very special.

How do memories of your own confirmation stand up against the confirmation services that you lead now?

+Mark: I remember my own confirmation as if it were yesterday. I remember going with my mum and dad and brother and sister in the car. I remember the journey towards the church and the bells ringing out, and the coldness of the night air. I remember the boys sat on the right-hand side and girls sat on the left-hand side. Girls in veils and boys in school uniform I think it was. I remember the feeling as the bishop talked to us and I remember him saying God will ask things of each of us because of tonight.

That was the beginning of vocation for me, and the sense of what God is asking of me, so I remember it very very well.

+Paul: My own confirmation took place when I was twelve. I do still remember it; but, as I often tell people at confirmation services that I now do, 'don't do what I do', because I stopped going to church about three weeks after the service. My confirmation felt like a passing out parade, not like a 'confirming in'. The whole purpose of the confirmation service for me is that it is an affirmation of a commitment to Christ and his Church, so it's a nonsense for it to feel like a passing out parade. But that's how it was! Now that was in 1967 and I think that's part of what the culture of the nation and the Church was. You were much more likely to go through confirmation and it was like a rite of passage, but it didn't really engage you with staying involved in church life.

I remember the bishop being hugely distant; I don't remember who he was and I know he didn't talk to me at all – personally before the service or after it. So one thing I try to do is to meet all of the candidates beforehand and I stay around for tea and coffee afterwards. Now that of course is a change of culture; in the 1960s you didn't have that. It was a mid-week evening, in a church I had never been in before. We weren't rehearsed . . . it was a catalogue of bad experiences!

+ **Mark:** I also remember that I didn't see the bishop before or after the service. There was no physical contact with him apart from the actual confirmation. That's why I do some of the things I do around confirmation in that I always ask the parish priest for a list of names of those I'm confirming and I keep them on the altar here in my chapel. For two weeks, morning and evening, I pray for them by name, and then when I've met them and confirmed them, I pray for them by name, this time with a picture of their face in my mind, for two weeks afterwards. I ask them to pray for me and I give them a card with my name on and a prayer – really what I'm saying is that this is something we are in together and that I value them praying for me. I meet them before the service and get them to tell me their name and I joke about whether or not they look like what I've imagined from their name. I ask them to just share a little bit with me about their journey; some of the amazing things I get told, awesome really!

People we have talked to have often reported how good it was that the bishop talked to them and was approachable.

+Paul: One of the things that has been invaluable for me has been asking candidates to write a little paragraph about themselves to send to me before the service. That means that in my preparation I have an idea of the age of the people involved, something of their own stories, which means I can gear what I say to respond to what they have written. I just feel I know a bit about the people I'm going to meet. It means that when I meet them, even if it's just for a minute or so before the service, I can thank them for their letter and have something to connect with them over.

+Mark: Some of the amazing stories I hear blow my mind because of the depth of insight and the clarity with which some young people come to confirmation; it just seems to mean so much to them. I confirmed one young man whose family had pleaded with him not to be confirmed. They'd offered him all sorts of inducements not to go ahead, and he stood up and gave the most powerful testimony. He could not have done anything *but* be confirmed.

Time and again, talking to these young people I come back to thinking that they have given me so much more than that which I have shared with them. Amazing.

What then do you think is the main role of the confirmation service?

+Mark: The main role of the confirmation service is, as I see it, the giving of a gift from a generous God who loves his children. There is no limit to God's generosity and that is so freely given in confirmation and the gift of the Holy Spirit – the sevenfold gifts of the Spirit. That sense of God believing in us and coming to us, confirming us in faith and for faith.

We might be forgiven for thinking that something like the liturgy for confirmation was put together in a dusty room, designed to tick all sorts of legal and ecclesial boxes, rather than to be a powerful and moving event. The notes that accompany the service, however, talk about the drama with which the service is designed to flow. We wanted to understand more about this dramatic flow, so we asked our bishops to walk us through the service step by step to help us get a grip on how it's meant to hang together.

The Preparation and The Greeting

+Paul: For me it's very important that there is an informal greeting and welcome before the service really gets under way. Most places begin the service with some kind of procession in, which creates that sense of drama.

Particularly where processing in is different from the normal church practice?

+Paul: Well it's different anyway because the church wardens walk in front of the bishop, and there's whatever you happen to be wearing. Even in churches where I haven't worn robes (which is very few) they still get the church wardens to walk in front of me as a symbol for them that this is the church officers coming before the bishop who has come here to perform this service. Then having had the liturgical greeting I like to include an informal greeting of my own, that includes a brief, simple reminder of why we are here, trying to mention the candidates by name if possible and then reminding people that the candidates are not the focus of the service: we are here to meet with God; the focus of this service is the living God himself.

The Collect

+Paul: Sometimes I use the confirmation collect, but sometimes the collect for the week makes more sense, particularly when I'm using it with the readings for that week. I tend to choose whatever is going to help the flow of the service best. The value of the collect is that is it good to pray like that right at the start of the service.

If the church is conscious that there might be lots of non-church people at the service they may go for the additional collects, which tend to be shorter, pithier and simpler.

The Liturgy of the Word

+Paul: Usually a church will choose either the Old or New Testament reading and the Gospel, and rather than using a psalm many churches will choose a song or a hymn, simply because of the length of the service. I encourage the hymns in the confirmation to be choices from the candidates.

Presumably you've sung 'Shine Jesus shine' a number of times?

+Paul: Quite a lot of times. And 'I the Lord of sea and sky' an enormous number of times!

The sermon is a very important part of the service, which of course it is whatever the worship is. My conviction is that the sermon must relate closely to those being confirmed but must also be relevant to everybody who is present. I am conscious that very often confirmation is a place where those who aren't used to being in church are present. So the sermon is part of sharing and communicating the gospel generally and connecting with those folk. So I want to say things that are going to help with the discipleship of those who are being confirmed, but also connect with the whole community.

I use the lectionary readings for that particular day and I do a different sermon for every confirmation unless it's a case of one in the morning and then one in an evening and then one during the week, although even then I will adapt and tweak what I say.

Using the readings for that week presumably keeps you from getting stale?

+Paul: Exactly. Inevitably I'm going to say a lot of the same things, I'm bound to say that reading the Scriptures is important and prayer is important, if you want to keep growing then these things are important. So I'll make a lot of those similar comments, just in different ways.

+Mark: I think that there are a couple of things that I say at every confirmation service and for that I make no apology really because, as I've said, you're only getting one chance at this. So whatever else I say in the sermon, I always ask them to remember this day. 'Remember how you feel just at this moment. And when the going gets tough revisit it.' I say it because of the memories of my own confirmation. I challenge members of the congregation to go back and look; 'When was your confirmation?', 'Who confirmed you?', 'Where was it?', 'What impact did it that have on your journey of faith?'

+Paul: I know some bishops who produce one confirmation sermon that they do for a month. I understand why they do that, they'll say 'during October this will be my sermon and these will be my readings' and then they do a new one for November. There's a high degree of logic in that with regard to the amount of time and energy that we have. I'm glad I've been able to do what I have done until now and when I move to being a diocesan bishop I'll just have to see what I can do.

According to the statistics that we've read, 50 per cent of the people you confirm will be young people. How do you make sure that sermon speaks to them?

+Paul: Well for a start reading their testimonies is so important, that way I can make sure that what I say ties in with what interests they have got. I try to stay in touch with their world, which at present with my youngest being only fifteen, means that I have found it easier to stay in touch.

You've read the Twilight *books then?*

+Paul: I haven't actually. But I know what they are. I do however listen to quite a lot of the music, I watch *Doctor Who* and I generally know what's going on in *Neighbours*, *Eastenders* and occasionally *Hollyoaks*. I don't need to know all of that in detail. I do, however, need to know something of that world and be able to reference it. And actually young people don't want you to pretend that you're part of their world. I'm an old man, according to them at least.

I never use the pulpit, rather I speak from the chancel step and I'll often walk up and down. That way I am pretty much at eye to eye level with the candidates, which makes it much easier to connect with the people I'm confirming.

Actually it's the same as communicating with people of all ages; it's about telling stories and making the Scriptures live.

The Presentation of the Candidates and The Decision. Have you ever been in a situation where you've thought someone was not ready to be confirmed?

+Paul: Yes.

How do you cope with that?

+Paul: The place where that is most obvious is in church schools where year 6 students have been prepared. There is no way in which I can know who is and isn't ready. What I can be fairly confident of is that there has been some peer stuff going on here. For some of them I'm in no doubt that this is deeply serious and for others they've just gone along with it because that is what the school does. I just have to treat everyone seriously; I have to treat them all as if they are taking it seriously. That's really the only setting where I think that's an issue.

At that point the bishop is reliant on those who have prepared the candidates. This is a partnership between us, so I come in on the understanding that they have been properly prepared and I suppose that is why the presentation is important, because effectively whoever is presenting them is saying 'We have prepared these and we are confident they are doing this for the right reasons.' I take that on trust.

The Profession of Faith. Do you get everyone in the congregation to do that together?

+Paul: I do, because I think it is really important to say that you share the same faith as the whole body, to remind you that we're all in this together. The good thing about the way it's generally done is that the candidates are still standing right in front of me so it still feels very much like a personal profession of faith to God, which the bishop can hear, but also they are doing it with everyone else together.

Then after any baptisms and the declaration for reception into the Church of England we move into the confirmation itself.

+Paul: There are various things that I do and I know other colleagues do as well.

I tend to confirm the candidates standing in a semi-circle rather than kneeling, I then go round to them rather than them coming to me. There is something for me about us both standing up and me being able to look them in the eye when I say 'God has called you by name and made you his own.' I want to demonstrate that we are equally Christian here. While I know that the kneeling is symbolic of kneeling before God, and I'm aware that this might be about me, it just feels a bit awkward. I'll do it if people want, but my preference is to talk to the candidate eye to eye, particularly as I tell them that God has called them by name.

That's my favourite phrase in the whole service. To look at someone in the eye and say 'God has called you by name and made you his own', that is a really powerful moment.

The whole individuality of the confirmation service is so wonderful. We could so easily confirm people en masse, but we don't, we take time out for everybody, individually, it's symbolic of our relationship with God.

+Mark: There are awful stories of times gone past when many hundreds would be confirmed in one service and of them kneeling at the communion rail and a plank being put across their heads and the bishop putting his hands on the plank and saying 'confirm O Lord your servants . . .', so they were all confirmed together. Now that's all gone, and this liturgy that we have now where you call them by name, 'Rebecca, God has called you by name and made you his own. Confirm O Lord your servant with your Holy Spirit', is so personal.

+Paul: By that moment I have got the whole congregation to sit down, and I encourage the friends and family of the candidate to stand up or sometimes when it's logistically possible to come and stand round the candidate.

I always, but always, do an informal introduction before the act of confirmation. So before 'our help is in the name of the Lord . . .' I always explain what is about to happen, which includes when to stand and so on. And I remind everyone that at this moment it isn't just me who is praying for the candidate, but that instead we should all be praying for them. Sometimes I use oil and sometimes not, depending on the tradition of the church generally. I place a hand on the shoulder and look in the eye for 'God has called you by name . . .', and then I place a hand on the head for 'Confirm O Lord . . .' If they are using oil, I will use it whilst I say 'God has called you by name . . .'

At this point I always stand there and wait. I keep my hands on their head. I don't move on very fast. I quite often share a verse of Scripture, and those are not pre-prepared, or hardly ever. In some traditions they might say that I was sharing a word of knowledge or a word of prophecy, I know that not many bishops do that; the only thing I can say is that it has been extraordinary the number of times that afterwards people have come up to me and said, 'You have no idea how appropriate that was.'

What the outsider sees and has regularly said to me is that they felt that moment made the whole thing very personal. They appreciate the way I have treated each person individually, and haven't said exactly the same thing to everybody.

+Mark: I remember confirming a girl who was fifteen and after the confirmation service, as I was signing books and what have you, her father came up to me and said, 'Just to let you know that I don't believe any of this bunkum at all; I don't believe a shred of it. But if anything could make me feel as special as you've made my daughter feel then I would have it by the bucket full. I looked at you confirming her', he continued 'and you made me feel that she was the only person in all the world that mattered.'

I always say to the parish clergy 'Do not look to me to rush', because I won't. This person will be confirmed once and they will know that the time has been given to them, so the hands remain in place for a significant period of prayer for that person. The marking out of the cross, all done carefully. Looking into their eyes; a sense of engagement with them and a confirmation. And to see that look, often a look of relief that the moment has come, is just awesome.

+Paul: On one occasion I also had a vicar writing to me a couple of days later to say that one of the people I confirmed on Sunday felt that they were healed while they were being confirmed. Now I have no way of checking that out, but the vicar said that it was something to do with their knee and the one thing they could tell me was that they were now walking more freely than they had for a very long time.

I'm very conscious that, whatever you say theologically, at that moment, the bishop is God's representative to that person and also the Church's representative. I am there, acting on behalf of the whole people of God, who are also standing at that moment saying 'We are with you bishop and we are with you candidates.'

It's a huge privilege, an enormous privilege. Which is why it never gets dull or boring; it's never just another confirmation. For these people this is their one chance to be confirmed.

This is something we've written elsewhere in the book, that this isn't something you can take another shot at. This is where you take on the mantle of the adult faith.

+Paul: Absolutely. As you know I'm a great advocate of children and communion and one of the pluses of that for me is that confirmation can wait. A lot of people used to be confirmed so that they could take communion. Confirmation now becomes a rite which is much more about 'I as an adult in terms of faith, am committing myself to Christ and to his Church.'

What is the Holy Spirit doing at this moment in the service? Is it akin to when Paul laid his hands on the followers who had been baptized but never received the Spirit? Or is it a case of every time we lay hands the Holy Spirit comes? What is going on?

+Paul: The Holy Spirit comes upon someone when they are converted to Christ. Confirmation is not the receiving of the

Spirit. The Pauline story is all to do with the growth of the Church into Gentile communities. That's why you have the incident in Samaria and the incident with Cornelius. They are bounded by the historical circumstance. Paul is clear himself in Romans and Corinthians that anyone in Christ is born of the Spirit. I think that confirmation is undoubtedly a commissioning for service because it is a very public proclamation and confirmation of your faith. You are saying to the world 'I am committed to following Christ.' There is an empowering and an equipping of the Spirit for that public service which, because of what the person is doing, they need, in a whole new way, to be aware of the Spirit. There is no doubt from what some have told me that it is a very tangible experience. People say that they feel completely different or they feel transformed, or that they've felt God's love in a way they've never felt before. They obviously have felt it before or they wouldn't be standing there. So I have no doubt that the Holy Spirit is at work, although I may not know exactly what he is doing. Why should I know?

The Commission

+Paul: Which I always request we keep in. I think it's hugely important because it utterly reiterates this notion that your confirmation isn't the end, rather it's the start of all that lies ahead.

I usually invite the whole congregation to stand and explain to them that this is their opportunity to reaffirm, in the light of all they have seen and heard, their commitment too. I invite them to join in the responses if they want to and I would say that I get a lot of response from that. Now some will just do it out of form, but others have said to me that it feels like the service becomes an act of committal for everyone who is present.

Is the commission putting words on what has silently already happened during the service?

+Paul: Exactly. I am conscious that there are certain texts that I use quite often when I am praying for someone and one of those is 'let the word of God dwell in you richly'. If you have said that over someone and then you ask 'will you follow in the apostles teaching?' you are doing just that.

The words of the commission are just rocket fuel.

+Paul: I wish they were mandatory I really do.

How do we make sure that a young person hears those words and realizes what they are being commissioned to do? Do you think that bit gets missed because it is simply more words?

+Paul: That is the danger. Some will think that we've already had loads of questions and answers, loads of words, and that we've already said all this in the decision. But this is so much more specific. It's about how you will actually follow this through.

    I suppose that you overcome the risk of it being lost in the way that you introduce it. You don't just go into it, but instead you explain it, and that need only take a couple of sentences.

    If you don't have communion as part of the confirmation, then the commission is a fantastic way to end the service, with just a moment of welcome and sharing the peace. There really is something very powerful about not having communion and just finishing there. You are commissioned to go out; we say you're welcomed, there's a big round of applause and then we greet one another and then finish.

If the choice was yours every time what would you choose? Would you have communion or not?

+Paul: I would vary it. I'm not wedded to one way or the other. Sorry.

Do you want to talk about the communion part of the service any further?

+Paul: I think the welcome and the peace are very important.

> There is one bit that I do that I don't know of many others who also do, which is I get the candidates to introduce the peace. So I get them all to stand up with me, we do the formal welcome, I get them to turn round, to stand with me and then to read the words of introduction to the peace. I tell them that they are the bishop for this portion. It means that they are still with me, so I can greet them, and then they can go off. It's a way of turning them round so people can see their faces rather than their backs and saying we are part of this together.

Reading the words of the introduction 'God has made us one in Christ' I can see why it works.

+Paul: It does. And I think it's powerful for them to say that that's what God has done for us.

> Lighted candles are used variably. Some don't do it at all, some do. For a lot of people it is quite valuable to have something like a candle to take away, but I always feel that liturgically I have some questions about it; especially if you use the commission. We have already said that we are going out into the world to do this, so why do we then again say 'shine as a light . . .'?

I guess it's there to remind us of the baptism.

+Paul: Absolutely, and as I've said, for a lot of people the physical thing of having a candle they were given on that day is very important. There's also a practical function for me, which is that if I have walked them out of the service, which I nearly always do, I can then stand with them at the back and say 'congratulations', 'well done' and whatever, and if they have candles I can suggest that on their birthday or at Christmas or on the anniversary of their confirmation they can light the candle as a reminder of what they have done.

However, if it wasn't there I wouldn't personally feel any great loss.

At the end of the confirmation service, what should the young person's overriding memory of that event be?

+Mark: I hope that they will remember the occasion, that they will remember that sense of being equipped for something and called to something. And that sense that they are being surrounded by a great outpouring of prayer.

+Paul: That they have met with God, not that they have met with the bishop. Not that they have had a great day, not that the cake was nice but that they have met with God in some way. And that they have a conscious memory of that being the day that they publicly said 'I am following Christ and I am part of his Church.'

Why does the confirmation service need the bishop's presence? What is his role?

+Mark: I think the bishop is there to represent the wider Church. Confirmation isn't just between a candidate and God, or even the candidate, the congregation and God. The bishop is there as the link or the symbol of unity, his presence says that this confirmation of faith is happening within the context of the Church universal; that this isn't a me-and-God issue; this is an *us* issue and we are together in this. My presence as the bishop simply says to them that we are together; we are that Church of God in all the land stretching between here and eternity. I hope the bishop's presence makes that tangible.

An old title for the bishop is 'defender of the faith' and he is certainly present in that role, but he's also there as chief pastor; he exercises a pastoral role, a teaching role and a praying ministry. It's a huge opportunity for bishops to encourage young people. One of the things I always say to people is that there are going to be times after today when being a disciple of Jesus Christ will be incredibly tough. You will be in places which will be very painful – at school, at college, at work. There will be those who will be ready to make fun of you, who will have a go at you because you're a Christian. Be ready and draw on the gifts that God is giving you in this moment to equip you to answer them.

What about the young person? What is their role in the service?

+Mark: I am time and time again full of admiration for young people. They are growing up in a world very different from the one I grew up in. The pressures on them are not as they were for me and the fact that these young people have made a conscious decision to follow Jesus Christ and be confirmed in that faith leaves me full of admiration for them. My encouragement to them in the time I have beforehand is very simple: don't be afraid; open your hearts to Jesus Christ tonight and let him, through his Holy Spirit, come and dwell with you. And that's what I hope and pray happens.

How can we get young people involved in the service? We've heard of churches outside the Anglican Communion who encourage young people to help with the writing of the liturgy for their confirmation service, is that something you could envisage happening here?

+Paul: It would be hard for them to rewrite the core elements of the liturgy, because of the commonality of what the liturgy is about. I think that young people also want to know that what they are doing is part of the norm and part of the wider Church. Perhaps there is a feeling that they don't actually want to mess around with the liturgy too much.

+Mark: We do have to respect and value and draw from the fact that in the service itself there is a given and the fact that everybody in the Church of England will be confirmed according to this rite is one of those givens and also unites us together in ways that transcend tradition, churchmanship or ways in which various bishops do it. This is the gift that we share in common and that's hugely important.

+Paul: I think the involvement in the choosing of music, of sharing testimony, of doing the readings and so forth is key. All of that gives them a great deal of scope to be shaping the service to some extent. I have had some examples of services I have done where we have pared the liturgy back as much as we can in order to fit the service into the young people's regular pattern. St James' Church, Shirley is a good example. The young people's Sunday night café church congregation is a regular part of that church's worshipping life so we asked how confirmation would fit into what is fairly normal for them. In that service they changed quite a lot of it.

It's worth asking if there are there friends and supporters who can be part of the welcome team at the service, or helping with refreshments afterwards, so that wider family and wider friendship groups are all sharing in the event. I think helping them in the preparation stage is going through the service and explaining where there are options and asking what the young people would like to include; asking them what they think the best way for the service to flow would be. You could ask whether they wanted to go to the font, or would they like to sign themselves or would they like their friends to come and sign them. There are all sorts of bits in the liturgy where the young people could be asked how they would like it to happen.

+Mark: One confirmation that I can think of, from a parish in the catholic tradition, as part of their confirmation preparation, had made a set of vestments for me to wear at the confirmation. That was hugely important because they were preparing for this big day and, as one of the young girls who I confirmed said, 'We wanted the best.' They made a chasuble and a stole, which I wore and which have now become my confirmation set, so every time I go I will wear that confirmation chasuble. I'm often moved where young people especially, because of their directness, do the bidding prayers and the things that they pray for and the way in which they pray for things is really important – lots of creativity.

+Paul: The thing I have learnt is that the service is flexible enough to do in a very high church with incense and all of that, but it is also possible to do it in a café style. You can play around with it in that sense. The core liturgy works in different settings, you just have to work with it.

Which is quite a testimony to the people who put it together really.

It might be difficult to pick up from the page but the feeling that we got as we spoke to Bishop Paul and Bishop Mark was a huge passion and love for confirmation. In fact whenever we speak to bishops about the subject, that passion is usually the first thing that comes through.

As we continue to explore mixed economy church in the Anglican tradition, we will need to keep reassessing the rite of confirmation. As new congregations reach maturity they will want to explore how to engage with the service in a way that suits them. It's exciting that, in these two bishops at least, we have people who seem willing to explore how best to serve those people who are making this new and bold stand for the Christian faith.

What is our advice to you as you plan your confirmation service? It's simple really: be creative.

It all comes down to speaking and listening. Speak to the young people, the bishop, the vicar, the youth leader, the parents and sponsors. They will all have something invested in the service. Don't assume anything; the bishop probably won't just want a dusty traditional service, the young people are unlikely to want rock music and flashing lights. Everyone involved wants the service to be as powerful and meaningful as possible for all involved. The worst thing in the world would be for the service to feel as if it was being done *to* the young people with them feeling as if they have no control over it or say in its contents.

The confirmation service provides an ideal opportunity for young people to explore what worship is about. Go through the service and the notes with them; explain what each section is for and what it means. Help them to get an idea of all the work and effort that has gone into creating this rite, the attention to detail and the desire throughout for that *dramatic flow* we talked about earlier. Getting them to choose songs and write prayers is only patronizing when it is reduced to choosing their favourite bit of music and reading heavily adult-edited prayers.

If we really believe that young people are ready to take on the promises of the confirmation service then we also have to believe that they can have a real and powerful input into how the service is conducted. For that reason we believe it is vital that they are consulted as much as possible about the service. It's sobering to think of how many young people (Bishop Paul included) came to confirmation ready to commit themselves to following Christ and left utterly disillusioned and disappointed. Consultation can only result in a better service. It has to be worth the effort.

Chapter 10

Post-Confirmation

Susie Mapledoram

What happens next? We've already talked about the nature of endings and the positives and negatives that can come from that, but in this chapter we want to explore that a bit further. When we come to the end of the confirmation preparation and our young people have been confirmed – what, if anything, do we do next? Or to put it another way, if we want to continue to see our young people grow in their faith, what can we do post-confirmation?

We return to our research and look at three key areas that have had an impact on the young people that we surveyed, draw some conclusions on the reflections, and then share stories of good post confirmation practice.

Susie's reflection

I didn't learn to drive until I was in my thirties and the novelty of being behind the wheel still hasn't worn off some years later. Much of my work involves chugging round my diocese, visiting youth leaders and clergy, and inevitably I am regularly making new journeys to new places. I've been brought up in a family that love maps and I'm no different. My dad must own virtually every Ordnance Survey map going and I have to admit that I'm a bit of a fan of maps and atlases and get slightly over excited by quizzes that involve capital cities.

You get the picture.

When I left my post with the Diocese of Blackburn my colleagues very generously gave me a sat nav (which I've named Sean) as a leaving present. Sean has been my greatest travel companion (apart from the times when he gets irritable with my unwillingness to make a U-turn in the middle of the M61). I'll set off for a new destination in the diocese and hang on Sean's every word as I weave my way round Rochdale, Bolton or Salford and rejoice heartily when I arrive at my destination. When I return to that destination another time I may well plug Sean in to be on the safe side, but I do have a fairly accurate photographic memory so the journey appears somewhat familiar and I may even attempt the return journey from memory.

There is something about going back to the places that we've been before. We remember that initial journey; the tricky junctions, the beautiful views, the landmarks, the buildings, the shops and arriving at our destination. It's significant. Then maybe over the weeks, months and years, we may well make that identical journey many, many more times, but the journey will always bring something new – roadworks, weather, stopping for petrol, an accident or picking someone up en route. I think that there might be a helpful analogy here for us in thinking about what happens next – post-confirmation.

The whole process of preparing for confirmation and then experiencing the service can be seen as an initial journey of exploration and arriving at a destination of discovery and declaration, but then what happens next? Does all that we have explored during our preparation just sit as a check list to accomplish in time for the confirmation service? Or do the areas that we've talked about, questioned and understood become landmarks on our faith journey that we return to over and over again, always seeing something new and fresh in them each time?

So what do we do? Give our young people a post-confirmation map and leave them to make sense of the rest of the journey and go it alone, assuming that if they've travelled the journey once they'll remember the way? Or do we continue to journey with them and revisit those foundations of the Christian faith as part of their ongoing discipleship and growth? We travel that journey of exploration in this chapter and look at why there desperately needs to be a post-confirmation strategy. We'll further explore our research and draw some conclusions on the reflections, and then share stories of good post-confirmation practice.

The journey

In the research that we undertook (referred to in previous chapters) there was a significant number of people who alluded to their experience of being confirmed as a 'step', 'stage' or 'marker' in their journey of faith. We've already talked about the analogy of journey and its helpfulness, and it seems from those who took part in the questionnaire, that this is a picture many can relate to. Comments such as 'I thought it was the next step in my faith', 'it seemed the right point in my Christian journey' and 'a marker in our journey of faith' would imply that their thinking is that confirmation is one stage of their Christian journey and that something would naturally come after it. Nobody claimed that this was the end of their faith exploration, so we can surmise that there is a real anticipation of something more beyond the confirmation service that will continue to enable them to explore their faith and grow.

Seeing confirmation as a 'marker' in their journey was another helpful and insightful analogy.

For some, confirmation was a defining moment, but for both positive and negative reasons. One respondent commented 'though it made a difference I don't think I was the biggest life-changing experience for me. I have moments in worship that affect me more than my confirmation did but it was the symbolic step that helps to keep me on track sometimes', another stated 'there was a point in my life when I stood up and declared what I believed in and in many ways it is still a reference point to my life today' and another claimed confirmation was 'a step on the journey. I discovered loads more since but I'm glad I took that step, it means I have made a commitment.' Obviously, people's experiences are different and a number of responses declared that confirmation was meaningless, insignificant and 'a mess', but for many it does appear to be a key moment in their lives, which they refer back to or recall and remember positively. Isn't it often the case when we reach a landmark that we are reminded of the next stage of our journey and we even use landmarks to trigger our memories to remind us whether its left, right or straight on. If confirmation is indeed a landmark, then we need to ensure that we have signposts clearly marking what comes next.

Duffy Robbins talks about signposts in his book, *This Way to Youth Ministry*, where he discusses the nature of incarnational youth ministry. He uses the metaphor taken from John White's book *The Fight* that suggests that there are two approaches to our witness to young people; the signpost model or the salesperson model. 'The difference between the two is basic: signposts point the way: salespeople try to close the deal'.[1] A salesperson will hold your hand throughout the deal until you have signed on the line and then they will leave you; once you've been confirmed, the salesperson sees their job as done. Robbins is convinced that the signpost method is the way forward; our role as youth leaders or clergy is to keep pointing young people to Jesus and on to further discipleship, taking away the pressure of the 'close the deal' mentality of salespeople and creating space to be. In Deuteronomy, Moses draws a wonderful picture of how adults should act as signposts for children:

> Love the Lord your God with all your heart and with all your soul and with all your strength. These commandments that I give you today are to be upon your hearts. Impress them on your children. Talk about them when you sit at home and when you walk along the road, when you lie down and when you get up. Tie them as symbols on your hands and bind them on your foreheads.
>
> (Deut. 6.5–8)

It is vital that we inspire and testify to our young people how much more there is to explore, discover and apply to our lives once they have been confirmed. If we do that from the forecourt of our second-hand faith car salesroom with a 'seal the deal' mentality then we just send them off with their car and map and hope for the best. The alternative is to point the way, acting as signposts for them to discover answers and deepen their relationship with God.

What next?

We were interested to know the difference, if any, confirmation had made on the lives of those who completed the questionnaire. There were a variety of responses, however three areas stood out for us in particular and caused us to think further about what happens post-confirmation. Those three areas were; taking Holy Communion, a changed view of their place in church and a new mandate on them to share their faith with others.

We want to explore these three areas a little further, first by listening to what young people said, then unpacking those thoughts a little before considering some ideas for helping your group to get the most out of those experiences.

Communion

'Taking bread and wine at church acts as a reminder to me of the promises I made.'

'I can take communion now.'

'I feel I can now take part in communion.'

'Being able to fully partake in the most important part of the service and being so close to God through the sacraments has made a difference in my life.'

'God made the difference. I take communion in C of E churches as a result.'

'I do feel that my faith is stronger and receiving communion every week really gives me confidence to face the days ahead.'

'I feel more open to God now I can take the blood and body of Jesus Christ our Saviour.'

For a number of our respondents, the significance of communion was the key difference confirmation made. It's a shame that, for some, confirmation was merely a ticket to take the bread and wine at communion services while, for others, this marked a meaningful opportunity to take part more fully in communion.

If your church practice is to use confirmation as a gateway to communion then you might want to consider some of these ideas to help young people fully engage with this new activity:

- Create opportunities to explore the meaning and significance of the bread and wine.

    - Spend time reading through the Last Supper passages in the Gospels. Ask the young people what they learned from them and what they say.

    - Get young people to bake bread for the church to take communion. Ask them what they learned about bread and how it felt providing for the congregation in this way.

    - Offer young people the chance to administer communion to others, either in a formal church setting or in an informal youth group setting.

- Provide occasions for young people to talk to older members of their congregation about what communion means to them.

    - Our experience is that young people love the chance to hear stories from others. Invite people to come and meet your group and tell them their stories, or even better get families or older folk to invite young people to their homes for a meal.

- Invite the vicar in and ask him or her to explain the communion service to your group.

  - An ordained person may be so used to what is going on during the service that they may not realize how alien it is for a young person. Ask them to explain the intricacies of the service.

  - You could invite someone from a different tradition or even a different denomination to explain what they do and to discuss how this differs from your own practices. You could even visit a different church to take part in their service.

- Ask a member of the clergy to come and lead a service of communion at youth group, demonstrating that we can meet and share together, anywhere.

  - The young people may think that holy communion is reserved exclusively for church on a Sunday morning. Taking part in the sacrament in a different place – the youth club, someone's house or on top of a hill – would be a great way for young people to explore the service more.

  - You could sometimes use different liturgy from the one you would normally use in church – maybe something from the Northumbria Community or Iona. You could even try ditching the liturgy all together and do a Silent Eucharist, or a U2Charist (google 'U2Charist' if this is new to you) or if you're feeling really brave, get the young people to write their own liturgy.

These ideas aren't meant to trivialize the Eucharist. It's just that familiarity can breed contempt, so to change some or all of the parts of an activity can cause us to look at it in a new light. You might find that the adults will want to try some of them out too.

Church

> 'I feel a more significant part of the church.'

> 'Feel part of my church.'

> 'It enabled me to become a full member of the church community.'

> 'I feel that I am a committed member of my church community.'

> 'I feel like a member of the wider church family.'

> 'It has permitted me to take on certain roles in the Anglican church (e.g. PCC member, preaching), that would not have been permitted without confirmation.'

> 'Most of the people at my church are quite old so I think they looked down on me as not really understanding the meaning of things in church, but now they see me take communion they know I know.'

It is clear that young people's place in church is very important to them, and belonging to and being part of a community is extremely valuable.

For some young people confirmation becomes a real badge of honour, giving them the confidence they need in order to stand up as full members of the church community. It speaks of their deeper commitment to Christ and his Church. How young people think they are viewed is important to them (even more than how we adults perceive ourselves) and a number of respondents felt that being confirmed had the power to change the way they were viewed by other, possibly older members of their congregation.

They also seemed to think that having a role in church was important, even if for a couple of them this was the only positive outcome from confirmation. More opportunities appear to open up for those who have been confirmed and this seems to be welcomed by those who have experienced it. I'm not sure that I'm comfortable with the implications of many of the comments we read. How the young people feel now as a consequence of being confirmed indicates that prior to this process they didn't feel part of a community. It implies that they didn't feel significant within their church and valued as a full, participating member of their congregation.

Consider some of these suggestions for helping your young people feel more involved in the church.

- Create a balance of valuing young people regardless of whether or not they have been confirmed.

- Try to help your group recognize the significance of the journey they have just travelled and explore with them how they can translate that into service.

- Ask the congregation to explore what the young people's place in the church might be.

- Ask the young people 'What would you like to do next?'

- Discuss with the young person's family (where appropriate) how the home can become a place of ongoing discipleship.

  - You will remember from the chapter on adolescent development how important the family is both in terms of faith development and adolescent development. Reminding parents and families that the home is the most important place for discipleship is really important.

- Ask the young person how they might need help to communicate their experience with their family and friends.

  - Encourage them to write journals or blogs about their confirmation journey, or if they are on Facebook to create an 'event page' for the big day.

- Help young people explore their gifts and their talents, and find out how they might put those into service.

–   Use a gifts quiz to help the group discover what their gifts are and then help them find ways to put those gifts into practice. The Network Course from Willow Creek is one such option or again just search on the internet for 'spiritual gifts quiz' and find one that suits your needs.

Sharing your faith

'It has helped me to commit to something I'm so passionate about.'

'It made me stand up for a faith a lot more than I did before because I invited some friends to it so they understood a bit more about it.'

'I have learnt to stand up for my faith.'

'I believe it has made me feel stronger in my faith.'

'Having made a public declaration of faith I feel braver talking about God.'

'It helped me to feel more confident with my faith.'

'It started my confidence to speak about God to others by making a personal choice very public.'

'I am proud to be a Christian and I try to speak to others about my faith.'

There are echoes of Westerhoff's theory here – a move from acknowledging a faith that belongs to no one else but me and now I want to do something with it. For many, the public declaration of faith and commitment to the promises in the confirmation service provided a spring board into building confidence in sharing their faith and putting it into action. I think we can conclude that a foundation of knowledge in the key areas of the Christian faith and the public witness to them in the confirmation service go a significant way towards giving young people opportunities for sharing their faith with their peers, and getting involved in church and community-wide activities of faith in action.

Here are some ideas for helping young people have more confidence in sharing their faith:

- Work with our young people in creating a variety of opportunities for them to put their faith into action in a physical way.

  - There are loads: litter picking, painting people's fences, visiting the elderly, gardening and generally responding to the practical needs of their community.

  - You may find that you can join in with bigger projects in local towns. Lots of churches use the May bank holiday weekend as a focus for their social action.

  - Your group may want to think about raising money for a good cause: sponsoring a child through a charity like Compassion is a great way for young people to make a difference in someone's life and to see that difference in action through letters and photographs.

  - Perhaps even consider a short term mission trip with your group. More and more groups are going away for a week or two often to such far flung places as Eastern Europe or Africa.

- Explore further with them the joys and sorrows of talking about being a Christian with your peers.

  - This may be as simple as you sharing your experiences of faith sharing, both positive and negative.

  - There are courses that help young people explore evangelism and how to share their faith. *Lost for Words* from CPAS is worth looking at.

  - Help them explore how to use social networking to tell their friends about their faith; it may be as simple as clicking the 'Christian' box on their Facebook profile.

● Continue to create opportunities for your young people to teach, encourage, pray and lead worship in your church.

  – *Get a Life* by Tim Sledge is a great course helping young people realize that they have a vocation and exploring what that might be.

Pete's reflection

There's a phrase in *Youth Apart* that on one level I disagree with completely and on another level I find really encouraging.

In what is generally an excellent (and underused) report there is a short section on confirmation. It states that 'Confirmation marks the integration of the experience of conversion together with personal development and heralds the beginning of a person's discipleship.'[2]

The first couple of times I read this it made me mad. The *start* of discipleship? So what had been going on in that young person's (or adult's) life up until that point? You can imagine my frustration.

And while I still believe that sentence to be completely wrong, it does have one saving grace.

At least it's the start of something.

We have already talked at length about the problem that confirmation has with being viewed as a passing out parade, and we have concluded that while confirmation remains the culmination of a course then if will only ever be a certificate handed to a young person to celebrate the completion of something. What we want to advocate is the reappraisal of confirmation as the start or even better the continuation of a discipleship journey.

This means the group have to keep meeting in one form or another. The person who leads the preparation has to keep up a high level of interest in the ongoing development of the young person, at least until they have been passed on to another adult who will continue to walk with them.

For too long, the sad reality has been that once a young person has been confirmed we breathe a sigh of relief, pat ourselves on the back because 'we got them before they left' and then start looking for the next group of potential confirmands.

In the first half of this chapter we hope that we have been able to show the need for confirmation to be followed by ongoing discipleship and support.

As Diocesan Youth Officers we have the huge privilege of being part of a network of people who are doing fabulous youth work and are working hard to support those working with young people. As well as encouraging continuing discipleship in parishes, many diocesan advisers host central events where they can draw together people who have been confirmed over a year to celebrate with each other what they have done. We asked our colleagues for some best practice stories and needless to say they responded with a host of creative and original ideas. Here are just a few examples:

Walk the Walk/Salt 'n' Light (The Diocese of Worcester)

Sarah Brush, Diocesan Youth Officer and co-author of *Moving Images, Changing Lives*

The young people of the Worcester Diocesan Youth Council wanted to encourage those who had been recently confirmed to continue in their journey of discipleship.

A few years ago they ran an annual day, inviting all those who had been confirmed in the diocese in the previous twelve months and giving them a chance not just to talk the talk of confirmation but also *Walk the Walk* of faith. On these days, the young people would organize games and activities to bring the young people together and grow relationships between young people of faith from across the diocese. The day was also a chance for the bishops who had confirmed the young people to meet with them again and encourage them in the outliving of their newly confirmed faith.

In 2008 the youth council sought to reach a wider group of young people both Christian and non-Christian through their event *Rock the Cathedral*, which drew 350 people from across the diocese to listen to young bands both Christian and non-Christian and to think more deeply about the spiritual side of life through the installation *Breathe*. The Bishop of Worcester also took the opportunity to encourage young people not just to 'Rock the Cathedral' but to 'Rock the World' with their faith.

In 2009 the youth council reviewed their need to encourage those who have been confirmed in the diocese and decided to run a new event to encourage young Christians (both those recently confirmed and others) to make their faith make a difference in the world. This is how *Salt 'n' Light* began, combining elements of both *Rock the Cathedral* and *Walk the Walk*. The young people themselves have planned workshops which through activity and reflection will help them put their faith into action, for instance making candles as aids to prayer, spending time considering their calling and making Christian wristbands to wear as a way to publicly declare their faith and reflect their recommitment. The bishop will also take part in the day to reconnect with the young people who have made their personal commitment to faith before him during the confirmation services around the diocese. After these workshops, designed to help young people reflect upon their faith and how they themselves are the salt of the earth and the light of the world, the young people will come together for a shared meal, an important part of our Christian community. After supper, the young people are going to take over a local church to worship with two of the bands that played at *Rock the*

Cathedral. This worship gig will include a message from a member of the youth council once again encouraging the young people in their faith within their own communities and also inviting them to be part of something bigger through work with the diocesan youth council.

For many young people in small youth groups around the diocese, both rural and urban, these events have had a powerful impact whether they have already made a commitment to faith or have seen the difference that faith makes to those around them. After *Rock the Cathedral* one young person commented: 'Before I went I was on the border of being a Christian and now I've decided to give my life to God.'

Giving space for young people who have been confirmed to mix with those still exploring has allowed people from both groups the chance to make important steps forward in their faith. Some have made tentative steps towards entering a relationship with God while others have taken leaps forward in their discipleship and service.

The Next Step (The Diocese of Derby)

Alistair Langton, Diocesan Youth Officer

The Diocese of Derby has been running a post-confirmation event called *The Next Step* since 1992 and its format has evolved and developed since that time. It is still a significant event in the Diocesan Youth Work calendar. *The Next Step* is held at the Diocesan Residential Youth Centre, the Peak Centre in Edale and attracts between twenty-five and forty young post-confirmands each November, around a quarter of all those who have been confirmed.

After the usual introduction and ice breaker game the weekend quickly gets round to listening to the young people's confirmation journeys. They share what confirmation meant to them and we explore what it's like being a Christian at school or in their local church and what difference it has made in their lives. We explore prayer and the other resources available to help them on their Christian journey. Worship is offered at several points during the weekend, with a range of styles and using youth leaders and young people to help deliver it. Many of the young people will encounter well-known contemporary songs for the first time at *The Next Step*.

Aside from the spiritual programme, the Peak Centre provides some excellent outdoor education opportunities; we take full advantage of these with hill walking in Derbyshire's Peak District, archery and rock climbing. These are most definitely a highlight of the weekend for our young people. The event concludes with a Eucharist with drama, music, prayers and items of liturgy written and rehearsed by the young people and with one of the diocesan bishops joining us as celebrant.

Our leadership team consists of myself as DYO, the Peak Centre Warden, and four volunteer youth leaders, plus a couple of young leaders (aged seventeen to eighteen) who are invited by the staff from previous *Next Steps* and are welcomed as full participating leaders on the weekend. It is an excellent training opportunity to develop leadership skills in young people.

Once we have met these young people they are invited to attend further diocesan youth events. The diocese runs approximately six weekends a year at the Peak Centre for young people from all churches, whether or not they have a youth group or have large numbers of young people. Over the years these weekends have spawned a loyal group of young people who support each other in the journey through adolescence and young adulthood. Many lose contact with their church but still return for the weekends at the Peak centre and others have naturally thrown themselves into becoming members of the Diocesan Youth Council.

The success of *The Next Step* depends on the co-operation of the clergy, the volunteer staff and the residential youth centre, all of whom recognize the value and significance of young Christians meeting and spending quality time with others from a diverse range of backgrounds.

The Gathering (The Diocese of Bath and Wells)

Tony Cook, Diocesan Youth Officer

The Diocese of Bath and Wells runs an event called *The Gathering*. This is an event for all young people who have been confirmed in the previous academic year. *The Gathering* commences with a mid-day picnic in the bishop's palace, followed by workshops, reflections, a Bible study and worship. We end the day with afternoon tea. The Bishop of Bath and Wells and the Bishop of Taunton are there all day and they both get fully stuck in. A number of youth workers from the diocese are also involved in planning and running the day.

The event is attended by about fifty young people; about half of all those confirmed in the year. Each candidate is given an invitation to *The Gathering* at their confirmation service and we follow this up with a personal invitation later in the year.

Young people who have attended the gathering can help plan and organize the event during subsequent years. In the longer term we plan to hold a residential gathering for young confirmands.

As well as *The Gathering* we are also writing materials for post-confirmation groups if they require it. This is particularly in response to needs in rural areas where the confirmation group is made up from lots of rural churches in a deanery.

After the event last year a twelve-year-old girl, the only young confirmand from her parish, emailed me to say that she had enjoyed *The Gathering* but that she didn't have a youth group in her church. She was hoping that we could help her set one up. We spent some time with them and they now have a youth group with ten to twelve young people in regular attendance.

While none of the above events can stand on their own as our solution to what to do with young people after confirmation, as part of a strategy they are clearly doing an important job. The strength of these events is that they encourage young people to get involved, they are opportunities for them to take up leadership roles and they provide a step into other possible activities. You will remember Michelle Guinness's disappointment with how Christians typically celebrate rites of passage. These events are testament to what we can do to join with young people to celebrate what they have done and as such we commend them to you as part of your confirmation follow up.

Resources

There are no end of good resources that you can use for your confirmation follow up. Some suggestions are provided in the Appendix at the end of this book. The most important thing to remember as you select what to use is that it needs to be the kind of material that helps young people keep moving on. As ever, the best sessions are usually created in-house. This is nowhere near as scary as it sounds; it usually means settling on a question that you want to ask the young people or a question that they are asking you and then taking bits and pieces from a variety of sources, books and videos that will help you all as you work through the answers.

In all likelihood your preparation for confirmation involved helping young people get to grips with some of the basics of the Christian faith: helping them go back over what it means to be a Christian, who Jesus is and what he did, and what it means to live an apostolic life. In short, you probably gave them lots of answers. If you used *Youth Alpha* or similar then this is almost certainly the case.

While there is nothing wrong with this, it's not really appropriate for the long haul. It breeds the idea that being a Christian is all about knowing the answers to questions, or that the Christian faith essentially boils down to an exercise in Bible comprehension.

A couple of years ago Rob Bell, founding pastor of Mars Hill church in Michigan, did a series of talks at his church entitled 'Jesus wants to save Christians'. One week he said that 'Jesus wanted to save Christians from having to know all the answers'.[3] This is such a useful reminder for those of us who feel as if this is what our faith sometimes gets reduced to.

It is far better, we feel, if the work you do with young people, particularly post-confirmation, helps them to explore and seek for God. To look for him in every situation. To learn how to discern his voice. To learn how to read Scripture for themselves. To learn how to ask questions and seek knowledge – you get the idea.

This is it, you see, confirmation needs to prepare young people for the rest of their lives. The preparation, the service and the follow up need to help young people find all that they need in order to continue growing in their faith.

Used well confirmation is an amazing tool. It certainly isn't the only way; many of you will remain unconvinced by its validity. For many an adult, baptism will remain a preferable rite of passage, or it may be that you have other ways in your church of marking a young person's passage through faith. But the principles in this book remain the same, regardless of how you choose to acknowledge them.

We hope that you have been challenged by what we have written and that you might do something differently from now on. Please take your young people seriously and if you currently prepare and confirm young people, then please don't underestimate the strength and the value of what you are doing.

Postscript: An Interview with Fuzz Kitto

'Fuzz Kitto travels the world collecting stories, creating stories and spreading rumours of hope. He is a youth worker, minister, trainer, speaker, writer and coach. His thirty-five years of being in ministry gives him a breadth of experience and wisdom for his consultancy work.'[1]

When we heard Fuzz was going to be in the UK we were desperate to grab thirty minutes of his time to chat about confirmation. He'd already inspired some of what we wrote in the chapter on rites of passage and we thought he would be a great voice for our postscript.

What follows is some of the wisdom we managed to glean from our short interview with the marvellous Fuzz.

What has been your understanding of confirmation?

When I was young we had Sunday School anniversaries and there would be a platform at the front of church. The young ones would be at the lowest level and the oldest ones would be at the very top. Each year we would progress up a step on the platform. The great thing about that practice was that we would always think 'one day we'll be on that top step'. Expectation and those symbols say to the children that one day this is going to happen to them – one day we want this to happen to you! We want you to find your faith; we want you to be able to tell your story, and tell us what God is doing in your life and to tell us what you want to invest your life in. We want you to explore the meaning and the purpose of your life and the mission that God's called you to.

Confirmation should be about confirmation of the great gifts of God – of faith and life.

Life is a gift from God and confirmation is a chance to give that gift back to God. Our response to God at confirmation should be one of realizing that this day is about how we action our faith as part of ministering in the faith community that we are a member of. It starts to help you to understand that there is something about the Christian faith which is not just about turning up to worship, it's a 24-hour expression, it's about loving God with all our heart, soul, mind and strength and loving our neighbours and loving ourselves. Confirmation expresses a deep understanding that this is about life, belonging, reality – and most of all about serving God as a part of God's chosen strategy – the Church.

I believe that young people are looking for ritual and looking for belonging. In faith development those are two key things that young people go through as they transition from teenage years into young adult life.

I think if we don't have rituals and if we don't have ways of celebrating steps of faith then we will not only lose young people, but we will see them finding and developing American Pie-style rituals of their own as mentioned earlier in the book. The place of religion in all societies is to answer the culture's 'why' questions and to be performers of the rituals. I think that is something very important and something that we need to continue to develop.

It's not just confirmation, we need to be developing other rituals as well; the beginning and the end of the football season, the beginning and end of the school year, when children graduate from junior school or when people leave high school. We need to celebrate those and have rituals for them, not only in the church but for churches to offer to schools and communities. The church should be saying 'we celebrate our young people' – they are now entering our community as young adults. When churches have a missional mindset they realize that their sphere of mission is not just the children who are part of our families or who come along to church, but to the 'parish' – which is all the people in a community.

We need to be asking how we help young people to understand that their faith is relevant. We need to help them develop a connection and a role that enables them to understand that they belong to the community and are important to it. Where churches have been able to do this we have seen a marked decline in youth crime rate, graffiti and an incline in community involvement.

I think we can also explore rituals for when people go through loss and grief. More and more in the USA and Australia and in the UK we are seeing the church being called upon when there is a national disaster and being asked to do some kind of ceremony to enable people to grieve. It is community sacred space. In young people's lives grieving is so difficult because of the blue skies they have – 'we're not going to die, we're going to live forever'. When a young person dies it's even more of a shock for their peers than for the peers of an adult when they die.

We can help when they go through sickness and particularly mental health issues, which has become the top area of ill-health in young people. What are the rituals we have for young people going through depression? Or going through the struggles of sicknesses? Where we can go to them and perform the ritual and say 'this a healing ritual', 'this is inviting God into your struggles, into whatever is going to happen, to journey with you, to be alongside you, to strengthen you and comfort you'. There is great opportunity to have a lot more rituals – life rituals.

Do you have any thoughts on how we might make confirmation more meaningful and life changing?

Charles Finney is believed to be the one who first started the 'altar call'. The way the altar call worked was that you came forward to the front of the church, or wherever it was that they were having the great crusade, to the 'holiness rail'. You gave your heart to Jesus and then you continued forward out the door to the hall out the back where there would be a whole lot of justice issues and social causes that you straightaway signed up for. There came a point in history, in some expressions of the Christian faith, where they stopped at the 'holiness rail', yet the whole point of what Finney and the great Reformers were on about, was that you gave your heart to God and straight away that had social implications. It had ministry implications and it had mission implications.

Tying the confirmation service together with the mission and the ministry that the confirmand has been called to helps them to understand that this is a real faith. We live in a time where we need to ask 'Does my faith work out in a real world with real people with a real God?' Confirmation says 'Yes, this is real. Yes, I'm giving myself to God.' Philip Aspinall, the Archbishop of Brisbane and Primate of Australia, said in his Synodical address in 2008 that we need to develop a missional understanding into our young people and include them more in the life and ministry of the Church. If we do not, we waste a great resource for the kingdom of God and leave young people feeling that faith is for when you are older.

This is why preparation for confirmation is so important.

I like to have someone who walks with you through your confirmation, a mentor. Some churches I know do confirmation through mentoring, so an appointed adult, someone more mature in their faith, walks with the confirmand so that through the confirmation process they have a companion. This companion is also involved in the confirmation service and often that person will give the confirmand some kind of special gift.

What we found in a number of churches that have this practice is that it is not only great for the person being confirmed, but it is so good for the mentor because they are having to articulate their faith and having to be asked questions, and that is such a blessing and gives that mentor a sense of 'wow, I actually have a faith to share'. It is such a privilege to nurture someone coming up through the confirmation process.

Some data has just come out of the USA which states that only 15 per cent of teenagers there have significant relationships with adults. There is an African saying that it's the parents that give birth to a child but the village that brings them up. What rituals can do and what confirmation does in particular is to offer an opportunity for the building of relationships with others in the church, it's a community expression! We can invite children in when someone is confirmed and say 'you were baptized, one day you'll be kneeling here, one day the bishop's going to be laying hands on you, the people are going to be celebrating this' – we can build a sense of expectation.

I also like to get each confirmation candidate to tell their story; why they have come to this point. A young person being confirmed needs to be able to articulate their faith. Some can write it up beforehand or it could be that the mentor or someone else writes it with them. Some may want to write a song, some may want to paint, some may want to cook and some may want to find some other form like dance as their way of expressing their faith.

I would get them to do a time line, like a lifeline, about the key points in their life and put it on display in the church, so it becomes a key thing that hangs there for a period of time that says 'here are the stories that we are celebrating'.

I heard of a church in the States where everybody at the confirmation service was given a bell and a piece of paper. When people come into the confirmation service they had to write on the piece of paper the name of the saints who had helped them to come to faith and supported them, not the canonized saints, but those Christian people who had incredible influence on them. They then pinned the name and the bell onto cloth banners. When it came to the prayers for the confirmation candidates these big banners were processed down the aisles from the back of the church to the front and as they processed they shook the banners and the sound of the bells was like the ringing of the stories of the saints. It gave the sense that these young people were in the midst of a great crowd of witnesses. They had a sense of being surrounded by the stories that God had created through people that had brought them and the church to this point and that one day they would also be a bell on those banners because they would be nurturing others.

We know you're a keen chef, does food play any part in celebrating confirmation?

What kind of good celebration do we have that doesn't have food associated with it? In Luke's Gospel all Jesus seems to do is eat, drink and hang out with his friends, and I'm thinking that's the Jesus I want to follow. In the Jewish tradition and many other religions there are particular special foods associated with special rituals and celebrations and festivals.

We need to develop confirmation food.

This might be particular dishes that are done, maybe by some of the many talented and gifted people in our church who express the art of food. When it comes to confirmation we could have these foods, which are confirmation foods, and when we taste that we taste confirmation. Every time we have a confirmation, we have a meal before or afterwards, and we taste it and we associate that taste with confirmation.

I'd do the same thing with smell. There could be a particular scent, incense or there is some perfume that is associated with confirmation. It works because scent is the most evocative stimulus for memory – followed closely by taste. It would be so good when we have a particular scent and think 'ah yes, that's confirmation'. The person who put together the Kerygma Bible study programme said that as Protestants when we took the incense out of the church, we didn't take smells out of the church; we actually allowed the mustiness to come back in. We need to displace the mustiness, with smells and scents that are about life. Confirmation should be enticing and all about celebration.

It would great to have a national competition to find confirmation dishes and drinks.

What would you say is the future for confirmation?

Everything that is important goes through continual renewal. We have seen that with faith and with worship, with liturgies, with mission, with justice and with evangelism. At different times and spaces within the life of the Church, things have had to be re-orientated and reinvented, or renewed or rediscovered. With confirmation we are at the point where this great ritual is about to play an emerging and crucially important role in helping people feel included in the Church. We've lost community in so many places and the Church is a community; a community of saints with God called to be salt and light to the world. The Christian faith is not an individualized, individualistic faith; it's a corporate faith. The Bible talks more about nations and cultures coming to faith than individuals coming to faith. In the individualized and lonely West I think we forget that.

What confirmation does is to give a person a chance to articulate their faith, it might be gentle, it might be powerful, it might be with tears or with a few stuttered words, but it gives the person a chance to say that this faith is important to them. We need confirmation to reflect that importance and we need to make sure there is an expectation that at confirmation something really special will happen.

My mother had an incredible gift, she knew how to advent. She knew how to build expectation for Christmas, Easter, God! With confirmation we need to build up a much higher expectation about what it is and what it's going to be, and that, maybe, God is going to do something through this process and celebration.

What we want to do with confirmation is to build it up as a very special occasion because it is! It builds hope and it builds a ritual that says to people 'we are included'. Why was Jesus baptized? He didn't need to be baptized. He comes to John for the baptism of repentance, but what was he repenting from? He associated with humans and he associated with the ritual that was there. He would have gone through the bar mitzvah and we know that he would have gone through the circumcision. For Jesus going through the rituals was part of being human, it was about being included.

Confirmation is about being included in the Church. It's a culture that we can develop. Building culture is one of the most important things we can do for all the important ministries and missions of the Church. In the future we need confirmation to help us to define the people we are – and that is so important.

It's the Nehemiah experience, building walls – with open gates – that say 'this is who we are'. Confirmation gives a church identity and when people know their identity it gives them the confidence to be the people that God has made them to be and to do the things that God has called them to do.

Appendix: Resources

Confirmation preparation and post confirmation material

While we would love to encourage you to try and steer away from becoming wholly reliant on published confirmation material, we are conscious that for many there can be real confidence found in using off the shelf. Our one caveat would be that we wouldn't want you to fall into the trap of thinking that the main purpose of each of your sessions was to get through the material. The main purpose is to help the young people meet with God and to learn more about the gospel. So if one of your activities sparks a (relevant!) discussion then let it happen. If one of the young people turns up to the group and they've clearly got some issue going on that they want to talk about, spend some time on it. And if you don't know the answer or they want to talk about something that you have doubts over – be honest, you never know you might find out more than you could ever teach.

Youth Emmaus 1 and 2 (Church House Publishing, 2003 and 2006)

In many ways *Youth Emmaus* is an ideal confirmation course. The first book covers much of the basics of the Christian faith and the second book encourages deeper discipleship. You could use this course and time it so that the young people get confirmed at the end of book one and then continue into book two after the service.

Moving Images, Changing Lives (Church House Publishing, 2011)

Is a film based course that seeks to help young people as they grow in their discipleship. It's innovative and because it relies heavily on film clips, most young people will find it engaging.

Youth Alpha

Youth Alpha is still the most popular confirmation preparation material for young people. It's a good introduction to the Christian faith and would certainly cover all of the basics. Be aware that Alpha has a habit of assuming young people are asking certain questions and then answering them. If they're not the questions your group are asking then you may want to question the usefulness of some of the session.

CY

CY is the youth version of the popular alternative to the Alpha course, with less emphasis on answering questions and more emphasis on grace. It's a useful resource.

Faith Confirmed (SPCK, 1999)

Despite looking like an RE textbook *Faith Confirmed* still remains hugely popular with churches preparing their young people for confirmation, with tens of thousands of copies sold over the years. It bills itself as an introduction to what Anglican Christians believe and provides a solid education in Christian beliefs.

Get a Life (Church House Publishing, 2008)

Get a Life is a course helping young people to explore vocation in its broadest sense. It's packed full of activities and would be a great post-confirmation course to help your group explore how to continue in their faith.

Nooma

If it's simply a discussion starter that you are after then you could do a lot worse than have a look at *Nooma*. These short and impeccably produced DVDs from Rob Bell, pastor of Mars Hill Church in the USA raise all sorts of issues in a well thought out, theologically reflective way. Young people love them, and you'll find lots to talk about.

36 Parables

Another good video based discussion starter from the US is *36 Parables* produced by Zondervan/Youth Specialties. These short videos are modern takes on ancient parables and will help you group rethink some of Jesus' teaching.

Obviously resources come and go all the time. The best thing to do is to keep in touch with people who can point you in the direction of the most up-to-date publications. Most dioceses now have a Diocesan Youth Adviser or Officer who will be happy to point you in the direction of some good resources and lots of dioceses have their own resource centres where staff will be happy to get hold of publications for you.

There are two good UK-based blogs, which regularly feature new resources: www.youthblog.org is maintained by Ian McDonald, youth officer in Oxford Diocese and www.dopcandy.portsmouth.anglican.org is run by Ben Mizen from Portsmouth Diocese. Dopcandy allows you to sign up for a weekly digest email so you get the information straight into your inbox. If you want to receive a monthly resource email from Winchester Diocese where Pete is the youth adviser you can email him: pete.maidment@winchester.anglican.org.uk and he'll add you to the list.

References

Introduction

1 Maxwell E. Johnson (2007), *The Rites of Christian Initiation*: Their Evolution and Interpretation. Minnesota: Pueblo.

Chapter 1 How Have We Got to Where We Are?

1 Ruth A. Meyers (1997), *Continuing the Reformation*, New York: Church Publishing Incorporated, pp. 1–2.

2 The Archbishops' Council of the Church of England (2006), *Common Worship: Christian Initiation*, London: Church House Publishing, p. 319.

3 *Common Worship: Christian Initiation*, p. 333.

4 J. D. C. Fisher (1978), *Confirmation Then and Now*, London: SPCK, p. 126.

5 Admission of baptized children to Holy Communion Regulations 2006, p. 190, http://www.cofe.anglican.org/about/churchlawlegis/canons/supplementary.pdf accessed on 22.07.2010.

6 John Stott (1990), *The Message of Acts*, Leicester: IVP.

7 Michael Green (1975), *I Believe in the Holy Spirit*, London: Hodder and Stoughton.

8 F. F. Bruce (1977), *The Book of the Acts*, London: Marshall, Morgan & Scott.

9 Bruce (1977).

10 Raymond Brown (1982), *The Message of Hebrews*, Leicester: IVP.

11 *Common Worship: Christian Initiation*, p. 6.

12 *Common Worship: Christian Initiation*, p. 187.

13 Mike Yaconelli (2001), *Messy Spirituality: Christianity for the Rest of Us*, London: Hodder and Stoughton.

Chapter 2 Rethinking Communion before Confirmation

1 Stephen Lake (2006), *Let the Children Come to Communion*, London: SPCK.

2 Leslie J. Francis and Jeff Astley (2002), *Children, Churches and Christian Learning*, London: SPCK.

3 Available at http://www.cofe.anglican.org/about/gensynod/ agendas/feb2006/gspapers/gs1596a.rtf.

For further reading

The Canons of the Church of England, London: Church House Publishing.

On the Way – Towards an Integrated Approach to Christian Initiation (1995), London: Church House Publishing.

The Archbishops' Council of the Church of England (2006), *Common Worship: Christian Initiation*, London: Church House Publishing.

Dom Gregory Dix (1946), *The Theology of Confirmation in Relation to Baptism*, London: Dacre Press.

David R. Holeton (1991), *Christian Initiation in the Anglican Communion*, Nottingham: Grove Books Limited.

Maxwell E. Johnson (2007), *The Rites of Christian Initiation, Their Evolution and Interpretation*, Minnesota: Pueblo.

G. W. H. Lampe (1967), *The Seal of the Spirit*, London: SPCK.

Ruth A. Meyers (1997), *Continuing the Reformation, Re-Visioning Baptism in the Episcopal Church*, New York: Church Publishing Incorporated.

L. S. Thornton (1954), *Confirmation, Its Place in the Baptismal Mystery*, London: Dacre Press.

Confirmation: *http://www.cofe.anglican.org/lifeevents/baptismconfirm/sectionc.html* (accessed 09.04.2009).

The History of the Church of England: *http://www.cofe.anglican.org/about/history/* (accessed 09.04.2009).

Chapter 3 Adolescent Development and Confirmation

1 Louise J. Kaplan, quoted by Chap Clark in *Starting Right: Thinking Theologically About Youth Ministry* (2001), Grand Rapids: Youth Specialties Academic.

2 Erik H. Erikson (rev. 1995), *Childhood and Society*, New York: Vintage.

3 Erik H. Erikson (1968), *Identity: Youth and Crisis*, New York: W. W. Norton & Co. Inc.

4 B. Inhelder and J. Piaget (1958), *The Growth of Logical Thinking from Childhood to Adolescence*, New York: Basic Books.

5 Daniel P. Keating (1990), *Constructivist Perspectives on Developmental Psychopathology and Atypical Development (Jean Piaget Symposium Series)*, New Jersey: Lawrence Erlbaum Associates Inc.

6 Douglas C. Kimmel and Irving B. Weiner (1995), *Adolescence: A Developmental Transition*, New Jersey: John Wiley and Sons Inc.

7 Kimmel and Weiner write that adolescence is the process by which adolescents are 'capable of separating themselves from their parents and thinking for themselves, while at the same time continuing to participate as family members and collaborating with their parents in resolving issues in their lives'.

8 Chap Clark, 'The Changing Face of Adolescence: A theological view of human development', in Kenda Creasy Dean, Chap Clark and Dave Rahn (eds), *Starting Right: Thinking Theologically About Youth Ministry* (2001), Grand Rapids: Youth Specialties Academic. This is a must read for anyone who wants to get a theological perspective on adolescent development theory.

9 John Conger and Nancy L. Galambos (1997), *Adolescence and Youth: Psychological Development in a Changing World*, New York: Addison Wesley Longman, Inc., p. 46.

10 David Hay with Rebecca Nye (1998), *The Spirit of the Child*, London: Harper Collins.

11 Kathryn Copsey (2005), *From the Ground Up*, Oxford: BRF, p. 36.

12 http://jmm.aaa.net.au/articles/19334.htm (viewed August 2009). Thanks to Alison Hendy for drawing this concept to my notice.

13 Blondin (Jean-Francois Gravelet) was a tightrope walker who shot to fame when he crossed the Niagara Falls on a high wire in 1859. His story, which has a message about stepping out in faith, has been used in countless sermons and assemblies. For more information visit the Blondin Memorial Trust website http://www.blondinmemorialtrust.com/

14 The Tightrope of Adolescence is taken from Chap Clark's chapter in *Starting Right*. Chap has very kindly given us permission to use this illustration in this book, for which the authors are eternally grateful.

15 Building on the writing of Erik Erikson, Marcia wrote about the identity development aspects of adolescent development during the 60s. He developed four basic phases: diffusion, foreclosure,

moratorium and identity achievement. James E. Marcia (1966), 'Development and Validation of Ego Identity Status' in *Journal of Personality and Social Psychology*.

16 Meredith Miller and Kara Powell (2008), *Riding the Highs and Lows of Teenage Faith Development, Identity Formation and the Importance of Moratorium*, http://fulleryouthinstitute.org/2008/11/riding-the-highs-and-lows-of-teenage-faith-development/
Fuller Youth Institute produce excellent resources for the study of theology and social science. Their website is well worth visiting.

17 This is not her real name.

18 Clark (2001), p. 56.

19 Miller and Powell (2008).

20 Kimmel and Weiner (1995).

21 Miller and Powell (2008).

22 Clark *et al.* (2001).

23 Miller and Powell (2008).

24 Cited in Richard C. Marohn (1999), '*A Re-examination of Peter Blos's Concept of Prolonged Adolescence*' in the Adolescent Psychiatry Journal.

25 Marohn (1999).

Chapter 4   Faith Development and Confirmation

1 Duffy Robbins (2004), *This Way to Youth Ministry*, Grand Rapids: Youth Specialties Academic, p. 384.

2 James Fowler (1981), *Stages of Faith*, San Francisco: Harper and Row, p. xiii.

3 John H. Westerhoff (2000). *Will our Children Have Faith?*, New York: Seabury, p. 87.

4 Westerhoff (2000), p. 88.

5 Westerhoff (2000), p. 90.

6 Westerhoff (2000), p. 92.

7 Westerhoff (2000), p. 98.

8 Westerhoff (2000), p. 94.

Chapter 5 Rites of Passage

1 Notes taken from training day with Fuzz Kitto at London Institute for Contemporary Christianity on Friday 17 February 2009.

2 http://reviews.media-culture.org.au/screens/pie.html (accessed 01.06.09).

3 Jason Gardner (2008), *Mend the Gap: Can the Church Reconnect the Generations?*, Nottingham: IVP, p. 89.

4 Peter Beilharz (ed.) (2001), *The Bauman Reader*, Oxford: Blackwell Publishers Ltd, p. 188.

5 Eric Erikson (1968), *Identity: Youth and Crisis*, New York: W. W. Norton & Co. Inc.

6 Lowell Shepherd (2002), *Boys Becoming Men*, Cumbria: Authentic, p. 10.

7 Arnold van Gennep (1977), *The Rites of Passage*, London: Routledge & Kegan Paul.

8 van Gennap (1977), p. 72.

9 Cameron Forbes (1984), *New Internationalist*, edition 138.

10 Unnattributed (1984), *New Internationalist*, edition 138.

11 Terry Pratchett (2008), *Nation*, London: Random House Children's Books, p. 14.

12 Maxine Green and Chandhu Christian (1998), *Accompanying Young People on Their Spiritual Quest*, London: Church House Publishing.

13 The Central Board of Finance of the Church of England (1995), *On the Way: Towards and Integrated Approach to Christian Initiation*, London: Church House Publishing.

14 Taken from the article, 'The Purpose and Importance of Rites of Passage', by Michele Guinness, published in *Bible in TransMission*, Spring 2008 and reproduced here with the permission of Bible Society. No part of the article may be reproduced, stored in a retrieval system or transmitted, in any form or by any means, electronic, mechanical, photocopying or otherwise without prior permission from Bible Society. For permission requests, please email permissions@biblesociety.org.uk or telephone Bible Society on 01793 418100. To access further articles from Bible in TransMission, please go to www.biblesociety.org.uk/transmission.

15 Jason Gardner (2008), *Mend the Gap: Can the Church Reconnect the Generations?*, Nottingham: IVP, p. 87.

16 From a presentation Anne Richards gave to a gathering of Diocesan Youth Advisers shortly before the publication of the book *Through the Eyes of a Child*.

17 Philip Fryar (2009), 'Heaven and Hell' from *Through the Eyes of a Child*, London: Church House Publishing, p. 280.

18 Andrew Root, *Immerse*, see: http://www.immersejournal. com/2010/02/20/the-confirmation-teachermentor/ (accessed 07.07.10).

19 Tim Sudworth (2007), *Mission-shaped Youth: Rethinking Young People and Church*, London: Church House Publishing, p. 87.

20 The Archbishops' Council Church of England (2006) *Common Worship: Christian Initiation*, London: Church House Publishing, p. 119.

Chapter 6 The Passing Out Parade

1 There are many definitions of what a young person is; the broadest definitions say that a young person is aged between ten and twenty-five years.

2 The Central Board of Finance of the Church of England (1996), *Youth Apart* London: Church House Publishing, p. 97.

3 The Central Board of Finance of the Church of England (1995), *On the Way*, London: Church House Publishing, p. 46.

4 Mark Yaconelli (2006), *Contemplative Youth Ministry*, London: SPCK, p. 147.

5 Mark Yaconelli's book really is quite brilliant and we can't recommend it to you enough. This paragraph is the summing up of most of a chapter. If it isn't already on your bookshelf you really must get it!

6 *Common Worship: Christian Initiation*, p. 119.

Chapter 7 What Does It Mean to Treat a Young Person as an Adult Christian?

1 From Chap Clark's chapter 'The Changing Face of Adolescence' from the book *Starting Right*, Michigan: Youth Specialties Academic (see Chapter 3, note 8 above).

2 Jo Pimlott and Nigel Pimlott (2008), *Youth Work After Christendom*, Milton Keynes: Paternoster.

3 *Respect? The Voice Behind the Hood*, Youthnet and British Youth Council, July 2006.

Chapter 8 Confirmation Preparation

1 'Confirmation training ever more popular in Finland', 29 April 2008 (The Evangelical Lutheran Church of Finland: http://evl.fi/EvLen.nsf – accessed 14.8.09).

2 Kati Niemelä (2008), 'Confirmation Training in Finland' Church
   Research Institute (www.evl.fi/kkh/to/kkn/rippikoulu/Finland_
   confirmation_training.doc – accessed 14.8.09).

3 Niemelä (2008), (accessed 14.8.09).

4 K. Tirri (2006), 'The History of Young Confirmed Voluntary Workers
   in Finland' (accessed 14.8.09).

5 Tirri (2006), (accessed 14.8.09).

6 The Evangelical Lutheran Church of Finland (2008), (accessed
   14.8.09).

7 You might be interested to know the contents of a 'drop of a hat'
   confirmation course. After some conversation with other leaders,
   quiet reflection and slight panic, I went with the following areas for
   this week-long course (four hours a day):

   Who am I and who is God?
   Jesus: human and divine, and his teachings
   The Holy Spirit
   Church
   The Bible
   Prayer
   The cross, repentance and atonement
   Resurrection
   Faith – putting it into action
   Relationships and self-esteem
   What happens next?

Chapter 10 Post-Confirmation

1 Duffy Robbins (2004), *This Way to Youth Ministry*, Grand Rapids:
   Youth Specialties Academic, p. 477.

2 The Central Board of Finance of the Church of England (1996),
   Youth Apart, London: Church House Publishing, p. 95.

3 Rob Bell's talks can be downloaded from the Mars Hill website (www.marshill.org) where you can still download this teaching series. Rob has also written a book entitled *Jesus Wants to Save Christians* (Zondervan, 2008).

Postscript

1 http://fuzzkitto.com.au/about/ (accessed 12.08.2010).

Index of Names and Subjects

Index created by Meg Davies, Fellow of the Society of Indexers